TIME AND HISTORY

TIME AND HISTORY

BIBLICAL AND THEOLOGICAL STUDIES

JOSEPH PATHRAPANKAL

Wipf & Stock
PUBLISHERS
Eugene, Oregon

Wipf and Stock Publishers
199 W 8th Ave, Suite 3
Eugene, OR 97401

Time and History
Biblical and Theological Studies
By Pathrapankal, Joseph
Copyright©2002 by Pathrapankal, Joseph
ISBN: 1-59752-195-7
Publication date 5/16/2005
Previously published by Asian Trading Corporation, 2002.

CONTENTS

Preface	vi
I. Reflections on Time and History	1
II. World History and Salvation History	23
III. History and Prophetic Involvement	45
IV. Mission of the Church in the World	69
V. Biblical Interpretation: Chance and Challenge in our Times	91
VI. Religious Maxims as Shaping History: A Study on Matthew 5:48	115
VII. God's Reign and World Religions	135

PREFACE

Jesus of Nazareth inaugurated his public ministry with a clear reference to the fulfillment of time (*kairos*) as the context of his preaching the nearness of the kingdom of God. He presented this new reality as a challenge which all were exhorted to receive through a radical change of their mind and heart (Mk 1:14-15). It meant that, as historically conditioned persons, humans have to read the signs of the time and respond to it in a meaningful manner in order to make their present and future salvific and fruitful. Writing to the Corinthians within the context of a critical stage in their history of estrangement and reconciliation, Paul said: "Now is the acceptable time (*kairos*), now is the day of salvation" (2 Cor 6:2). With the dawn of a new millennium, humankind has become more aware of the meaning and challenge of time and history, precisely because it is in and through time and history that humans have to build up their destiny and their future. At the same time, the euphoria and the optimism of the new millennium was radically disturbed and shaken through the horrendous event of September 11, 2001 which once again brought in an awareness to the human community that, in spite of a lot of good will and understanding, there is so much evil still lurking in the heart of humanity. Hence there arose a certain amount of skepticism and pessimism, and a consequent uneasiness about what time would bring in its train if it is not understood and approached in an elevated manner.

In our age which is characterized by the progress of science and technology, on the one hand, and consumerism and pragmatism, on the other hand, the reality of time is often approached and understood in terms of its utility and its capability of production and consumption and any time that is not productive is seen as meaningless and useless. Though time is the most precious gift humans have received during their pilgrimage of life on this planet earth and it is that basic reality within which human life and human enterprises are conceivable, we seldom take this reality seriously until we are confronted by a critical time in which a decision is to be taken or something important is to be done. Time as such does not mean anything until we make use of it and make meaning out of it either for oneself or for others. There are those who spend their time conceiving evil and executing their evil plans for the destruction of others, while there are also those who make use of their time for the good of the world and for the progress of humanity. The decisions for both of them are taken in the minds of humans. We have had enough of good and bad effects of these different approaches to time in the course of history.

History is the product of time that has gone behind us. Though it is clear to everyone that we are the product of personal and social history, history as such receives very little attention in contemporary thinking and living. Here again the pragmatic aspect has overshadowed the inner meaning of history. History is seen as something of the past and consequently, unrelated to the present and meaningful only for those who are interested in historical investigation. History is not only of the past, nor is it the study of the past in itself. It is the ongoing convergence of the past, present and future in the now which makes history and invites people to live in it and learn from it. A person without a sense of history, a society which is ready to forget its own history, and a nation devoid of a commitment to history are sure to experience total or partial frustration. It is the past that prepares the present, and it is the present that moulds the future and there is always an inter-connectivity between these three parameters of time and its progressive march.

Time and history play an important role in biblical and theological discussions in our times. The Old Testament is a record of history, remembered, reflected on and recited by generations of people till they received their present shape. The New Testament is also the record of remembered and proclaimed history. In fact, it is from the Bible that we get a great amount of insight into the meaning and message of time and history. Hence a reflection on the meaning of time and history in the Bible both from biblical and theological perspectives is important and necessary. These reflections help us to bring together the past and the present and enable us to face the challenge of the future.

Most of the material in this book was presented and discussed during a series of lectures delivered by the author in the Swedish Theological Institute in Jerusalem in October-November 2000 and it has been revised and edited to suit the present work. I take this opportunity to thank Prof. Tord Fornberg, Associate Professor of New Testament, University of Uppsala, Sweden, for inviting me to deliver these lectures at the Swedish Theological Institute, Jerusalem during the Jubilee Year which coincided with the jubilee year of my Religious Profession. I am also very grateful to Tyler Stewart for taking up the publication of this book from the United State of America.

Joseph Pathrapankal cmi

I

REFLECTIONS ON TIME AND HISTORY

It was an unusual and, at the same time, a very inspiring thing that happened on May 31, 2000 at the opening session of the *Katholikentag* in Germany, when to each one of the about 40,000 people assembled in the large square of the Town Hall of Hamburg a small sand glass was given and all were asked to hold it vertically for a minute and see the sand flowing from the upper part of the glass bulb to the lower one. Once this exercise was over, all were asked to turn to their neighbours who were standing on their side, relate themselves to these people, and take time to greet each other very personally and cordially, though right at that time they were just strangers. It was in this manner that the 94th *Katholikentag* of the German Catholics was inaugurated, which had as its working theme: "His is the Time" (*Sein ist die Zeit*). It meant that time belongs to God and that it is not any human making and humans are not expected to use it the way they want and like. They have to use it with a sense of responsibility and dedication. The inner message of the whole thing was that time is God's most precious gift to the humankind which all have to share with others and not enjoy all by oneself.[1] In the same way as people share their energy, resources, love, and many other things with others, perhaps from a more radical perspective, they have to share their time with others to help them, empower them, guide them and encourage them. It is time that is transformed into energy, resources, love, and compassion. As individuals, circumscribed by space and time, humans tend to make use of their time for their own selfish purpose; but as persons, they are invited to transcend these limitations and spend their time for the good of others. The choice between these two approaches lies with the humans, and it is a challenge which all have to keep on facing and to which all should respond meaningfully.

It is evident to all that the ongoing flow of time is the very substance and reality of human life on this earth. In other words, human life in this world is the sum total of time from birth to death. In fact, time is also the most challenging reality God has given to the humankind as a whole and to each individual person, through which all have to exercise the gift of their manhood and womanhood as they continue to live on this earth. Good as well as bad deeds are performed by making use of one's time, decisions are taken in the process of time and it is these decisions and their execution, in turn, that effect, affect and transform the course of life for everyone. The success or failure of all humans is decided by the

---

[1] Cf. G. Mlakuzhyil, "The Assembly of Catholics: A New Way of Being Church" *Vidyajyoti* 64(2000) 618.

meaningful or irresponsible use of this gift of time. But this most precious of gift of time is given to humans not as a lump, rather through a series of moments, demonstrated by the ticks of watch and clocks, right from the time of their being born into this world till the time they would breath their last. It means that beyond death there cannot be any more time. Time is the enriching context and environment in which humans have to celebrate their life in this world. The specific characteristic of human life is that it is a convergence of spirit and matter fused into one holistic reality. While matter provides life with time, the spirit, which belongs to the realm of the divine, has to transform time into a meaningful reality through its conscious involvement. The committed relationship of humans to time is an essential factor that determines the nature and outcome of human existence both for the individual person and also for the whole humankind.

It is the ongoing flow of this reality of time that is taken care of by humans at various levels that eventually makes history of one kind or the other. Individual persons, families, nations and humankind as such have their own history. Even as all of them continue to make their own history, the very same history is radically influencing them and transforming them in their historical march. Hence a new awareness of history is taking shape in our times, and all are exhorted to develop a new sense of appreciation of and approach to time and history. Here it is question not of a philosophical or scientific understanding of history; but rather of a realistic, humanistic and existential approach to history. After having spent much of their time and energy for the achievement of their selfish and aggressive gains, conquest of the continents, and plundering and acquisition of wealth during the colonial periods and the two World Wars, Europe and the entire West are becoming more and more aware of the need of a just, fair, right and meaningful use of their time for the emergence of a better history and for the creation of a better human society. It is an awareness that is really rewarding and it is something that the various nations in the world would better emulate and benefit from in order to create a new world order characterized by peace and justice. It serves also as a caveat to the onslaught of globalization which is a new form of colonialism, both economic, political and cultural. It would seem that the powerful nations of the world would never completely give up their economic, political and cultural might. Since the destiny of the world in our times is decided more by political powers than by religious principles, there is need of constant reminders addressed to the world leaders from religious circles which make clear to them that the future of the world is decided by a better and meaningful utilization of time that God has given to humanity.

The *Katholikentag* of 2000 celebrated in Germany was perhaps a reminder to the German Catholics and to all nations about how they have to evolve a new culture of sharing time and energy for the progress of the people and for peace and justice in the world. There had been enough of exploitation and the destructive use of time in the past, and Hitler's Germany has played a very scandalous role in it, which nobody now approves of. Now it is the duty of all nations to give up all forms of destruction and exploitation and to embark on a constructive and creative use of time and the making of a history that will be beneficial to the whole humankind. Equally important for the humankind is a new awareness that a certain careless, passive and uncommitted understanding of time is also something that is to be given up in favour of a more involved and constructive utilization of time through a culture of hard work, because only through this approach could progress and prosperity be achieved. There is no point in the developing countries blaming the developed nations because much of the social, economic and cultural development among them is the result of their hard work and perseverance during the past. The tall claims India makes about it being the largest democracy in the world as well as a secular state where all religions are treated on the basis of equality belie the equally appalling scenes of a lack of work culture, corruption at the top levels and communalism eating into the very fabric of political and socio-economic structures.

Dynamics of Time from a Biblical Perspective

When we speak about time and history[2] as biblical concepts, it is important that we abandon our modern scientific interpretation of these concepts, namely, time as a frame within which events take place, as an empty space or as a prior entity which is subsequently filled out with the ordered succession of temporally distinct events which make up history. It may also be noted that the biblical concept of time is very different from the mythological ideas of time found in the Ancient Near East, determined as they are by the cycles of the stars and yearly seasons. In these mythological conceptions, time is thought of in terms of cycles of time and history as returning endlessly to their starting points. Alien to the Bible is also the present-day conception of a purely linear time and history, according to which time is thought of as a straight line of limitless extent which, viewed from the present, extends backward through past events and forward through future events. A careful analysis of the linguistic usage of the Old Testament and New Testament with regard to time and related concepts will reveal the unique character of these concepts in biblical thought. At the same time, care must be taken lest theological arguments are built up exclusively on some tenuous grounds of lexical and grammatical structures of some Hebrew and Greek words.

---

[2] 'History' is a Greek word and it means an 'enquiry', the kind of intellectual exercise which the Greeks practised. The verb *historein* occurs only once in the New Testament in Gal 1:18. It relates to Paul's having gone to Jerusalem to 'get to know' Cephas, presumably with a view to acquainting himself with the historical facts of the Christian story from the best available source.

Important among the biblical words for time are the two Greek words *chronos* and *kairos*, both translated as time.[3] There is much disagreement among New Testament scholars about the inner meaning of these two words. On the one hand, we have scholars who maintain a clear distinction between the inner content of *chronos* and *kairos*, and, on the other hand, there are others who are totally opposed to any such distinction. Thus J.A.T. Robinson argues for a fundamental difference between two ways of regarding the whole of the time process and he holds the view that "it is a difference which the biblical writers indicate by their use of the two Greek words for time, *kairos* and *chronos*". According to him, *kairos* is time considered in relation to personal action, in reference to the ends that are to be achieved in and through it. *Chronos*, on the other hand, is time abstracted from such a relationship, time, as it were, that ticks on objectively and impersonally, whether anything is happening through it or not. It is time measured by a chronometer, not by purpose, momentary rather than momentous.[4] The same kind of a difference is adhered to by J. Marsh and some others. But such a clear distinction is totally rejected by J. Barr and A.L. Burns.[5] "I do not think that the attempt to find a profound significance in the New Testament use of the word *kairos* for 'time' or belittling the use of *chronos* in the New Testament will stand a close examination".[6] It is true that lexicographically a clear distinction may not be always valid, for in Mk 1:15 and Gal 4:4 both dealing with one and the same theological context of the fulfillment of the divinely guided time, we have *kairos* in the first case and *chronos* in the second case. At the same time, it cannot be doubted that there is some lexicographical sanction for the assumption that *kairos* carries with it some more theological nuance. It denotes in many cases the time which has as its content the work of Jesus (Matt 26:18; Jn 7:8) and the decision of humans to accept or reject this salvific event (2 Cor 6:2). In the *kairos* the gift of God and the demand that humans shall lay hold of this offering of salvation on God's part is brought home to humans in a definitive and unrepeatable manner (Lk 19:44; Jn 7:6) and for this the *kairos* of God gives certainty. In this respect it is unlike cosmic or human *kairos* which has to remain in a constant state of readiness for all possible opportunities even when they are only remote.

That the Greek word *kairos* carries with it this specific meaning is not a mere invention of any New Testament scholar is proved by the application of the very same semantic principle underlying the Greek usage. The linguistic development of the term clearly suggests that the basic sense is that of the

---

[3] Cf. R.E. Cushman, "Greek and Christian views of Time" *Journal of Religion* 33(1953) 254-264.

[4] J. A .T .Robinson, *In the End God* (London: Fontana, 1968). P. 57.

[5] Cf. A.L. Burns, "Two words Time in the New Testament" *Australian Biblical Review* 8(1953) 7-22.
[6] *Ibid.* p. 8.

"decisive or crucial place or point" whether spatially, or materially or temporally.[7] "The time of Jesus is *kairos* and so is a time of opportunity. To embrace the opportunity means salvation; to neglect it is disaster. There is no third case.... The time of Jesus was thus fraught with great issues".[8] According to the New Testament this decisive point is coupled with the idea of the gracious goodness of God in the gift of the *kairos*, challenging humans to respond to the gift of salvation time. Thus the seriousness and challenge of decision, already present in the Greek concept of *kairos*, is given an intensity and urgency which we find unique both in the religious proclamation of Jesus of Nazareth narrated in all the Gospels and in the moral demands and exhortations of Paul in his letters to the various Christian communities.

Time and History in relation to Eternity

A unique characteristic of time, understood whether as *chronos* or as *kairos*, is that it is available only to humans, and that, too, only during their life in this world. Beyond this world there is no more time. Time is therefore the very law of human existence and it is also the context of human life in its ongoing process. Hence time is the locus of human progress and growth. In this process of growth, time implies both past and future, which are converged in the present. This is what we have to understand as the essence and matrix of human history. History is the ongoing and dynamic process of time. But history, from the point of view of common sense, is the recalling of past events that are recoverable from the memories of people or from recorded annals of writings of historiographers or traceable from reminiscences of living traditions of people. Here we are speaking about a larger and more comprehensive meaning of history as the convergence of time with its inner dynamics. It means that time and history are interactive and intertwined. In this sense history is not understood merely as a series of past events where humans are only onlookers, but as a process of humans' making or unmaking of themselves in their dynamic relationship within the reality of time.

Humans, when they live on this earth, are temporalized and, at the same time, they experience also a trans-temporal dimension as part of their life. Being in time and history also means the ability and need to transcend time and history, and thereby to grow towards something beyond time and history, which we understand as eternity. What is significant about all human history is that it is something that leads to a finality that is beyond time and history. It means that, even as historicized persons, humans have to live in time and also transcend time and move towards the timelessness of eternity. Time and history are the

---

[7] Cf. Art. "kairos" in *ThDNT*, Vol. III, p. 455.

[8] Cf. Art. 'Time" in *A Theological Word Book of the Bible*, A. Richardson (ed) (London: SCM Press, 1950). P. 252.

experiential dimensions of humans, through which they have also to train themselves to participate in the eschatological meaning of eternity. This is done not by denying time or escaping from time, but by creatively participating in time, making the best use of time for oneself and for others.

Quite different from the concept of time and history is that of eternity. The Greek word *aion,* meaning eternity, has special nuances in biblical usages. Whereas for Greek thinking in its Platonic formulation there exists between time and eternity a qualitative difference, to primitive Christianity eternity is time itself in a new form. In other words, what we call time is nothing but a part, defined and limited by God, of the same unending duration of God's own eternity. We usually conceive of time and eternity as abstract and independent realities: time as a framework within which events take place, as if it is an empty space which is subsequently filled out with the ordered succession of temporally distinct events, and eternity as an endless time or timelessness. But basic to the understanding of time and eternity as biblical concepts is the fundamental idea that time is essentially understood from the point of view of time-content and eternity is also to be understood as the sum total of God's intervening in the history of humankind. In primitive Christianity eternity was understood as time itself in a new form. What we call time is nothing but a part, defined and limited by God, of the same unending duration of God's time which we call eternity.

If we discount the vague scriptural use of 'eternity' to indicate a very long duration, we can distinguish in general three uses of this concept. Firstly, eternity is understood as unlimited time, which is the manner in which the unreflecting mind represents the eternity of God. It represents a constant temptation for many people to understand eternity. Secondly, eternity is conceived of as timelessness and it is an eternity understood in an abstract sense. Thirdly, eternity can be conceived of as real duration that transcends time, insofar as it negates the essential characteristics of time, namely, its division into moments. This is the decisive notion of eternity as without beginning and end, as always total and simultaneous. Eternity is not a duration stretching out interminably, but a duration which in its entire length is gathered into one single moment. In this sense eternity is only another name for the unchangeableness of God. In a deeper sense it means that the absolute being transcends the entire order of beings and that it excludes in its unending living density any division, limitation or measure.[9] Eternity, as a concept, is difficult to comprehend. To go beyond time appears to humans more mysterious than to go beyond space. Temporality appears to penetrate our thinking in a much deeper way, so that we can only think of eternity as a reality which occurs in time. We are not eternal, but there is within us something which points to the eternal and which enables us to conceive of the eternal not merely as a negation. Seen from the perspective of a radical dualism,

---

[9] Cf. Art. "Eternity" *Sacramentum Mundi* (Bangalore: Theological Publications in India, 1975) pp. 249-252.

eternity and time have no relation one to the other. They can only be joined together by the doctrine of faith in creation, considered under the aspect of participation, which considers eternity as the origin, ground and measure of time. Time is contained in eternity not as though it were contained in a longer period of time, but as something from which time derives its being and unity, something which holds together time. Eternity is both that which gives rise to time and that from which time ceaselessly flows, and also that which bestows upon time its ultimate meaning and teleology.

Dynamics of History

It is important to realize that humans are the only creatures who can at the same time live in history and also make history which is the story of their being and becoming in time. Historians today recognize that there is no abstract and non-interpreted history. History is not a series of naked facts arranged in chronological order like beads on a string. An event is a meaningful happening in the life of an individual or a people. And history is the narration of these experienced events, events so memorable that they are preserved in the memory of the individual and the people and eventually written down in records. Obviously, historians do not report everything what has happened. Their narration is selective. They recount and interpret only those events which are meaningful and relevant to them or to the community which they represent. Some events have only a private meaning while others have a public meaning. The complex story of the struggle for the independence of India is a typical event which has a public meaning for the whole of India and for all Indians, past and present. But this inner meaning can be understood and appreciated only by those who are aware of the role it played in the history of India during the succeeding years. While some may be tempted to dismiss these events as having no relevance for them, others can see a greater meaning for these events insofar as they understand the entire meaning of the struggle for independence in a circle of faith and patriotism, without which the India of today could not be conceived. Denying the past precisely because it is past is the folly of those who do not appreciate the roots of their existence. People who are led only by pragmatic considerations are easily tempted to forget the meaning of the past. It is a question of forgetting the roots when they are reaping the fruits. Without the roots there would be no fruits either. Taking time and history seriously points to a new understanding of reality and of the place of humans and their role in them in terms of the creative possibilities of human existence. So history is not to be understood merely as a series of past events where humans are merely spectators but as a dynamic process of their own making or unmaking of themselves in their dynamic relationship within the reality and challenge of time in which they find themselves.

In this dynamic and ongoing process time and history are often understood as a linear and irreversible process. But it is to be kept in mind that there are also other and equally powerful models of history which are also to be taken into account if a comprehensive understanding of and approach to history is to be gained. The Christian view of history portrays time as moving from a beginning toward a goal, a fulfillment, whereas the Oriental and Greek concept of time was understood as a cyclic recurrence, patterned on the cycles of the nature and its seasons. Accordingly, theologians started contrasting the Christian concept of time and history with other perceptions, stating that with Christ's incarnation God himself has entered the wrongly understood circular time at a certain point, and with his whole weight of eternity has stretched out this time-circle and gave the time-line a beginning and an end, and thereby also direction and purpose.[10] In the context of this Christian claim to a better understanding of history it is useful to look at the various perceptions of history as we have them articulated in the course of human history among peoples and in various religions. Moreover, in Christian thinking there is a strong rejection of mythology as the opposite of history and consequently Christianity is claimed to be the only historical religion while other religions are involved in the cycles of mythology. In fact, according to many modern Christian theologians, mythology is the beginning of theology. The basic difference between theology and mythology is that while theology derives its premises from the data of revelation and human understanding of this divine event, mythology tries to explain things from observations and also from principles derived from reason and common sense. Hence history, mythology and theology are all inter-connected and complementary. The attitude of the Bible towards mythology will be explained later.

Models of History

History is basically a process and a movement. This process and movement aspect of history has been the object of much reflection and research throughout the history of humankind and it has received various articulations in the form of the cyclic, the dialectical and the linear concept of history.[11] The cyclic concept of history is said to be characteristic of archaic people, pre-modern generations, primitive cultures, oriental peoples, agricultural civilizations and the popular masses in general. Time and history are experienced and represented as periodic and repetitive and moving cyclically. This concept has its basis in the obvious rhythm of the cosmos and of living things. The endless succession and alternation of sunrise and sunset, winter and summer, the phases of the moon, childhood and adulthood, seed and tree, day and night illustrate the cycle of nature. There is a periodic regeneration of life which points to a periodic

---

[10] C. T. McIntire (ed) *God, History and Historians* (New York: Oxford University Press, 1977) p. 81.

[11] Cf. Samuel Rayan, "Models of History" in *Jeevadhara* 45(1978) 5-26.

regeneration of time. This means a repetition of the cosmogonic act. Cosmogonies, cosmic myths and primordial personages became archetypes and models for ancient humans. On them it patterned its life, laws, rituals, and all its movements and concerns. Thus the pre-modern human life was a "ceaseless repetition of gestures initiated by others".[12] The result is the idea of the eternal return, "the cyclic return of what has been before. Hence for the archaic humankind everything begins over again at its commencement every instant. The past is but a prefiguring of the future. No event is irreversible and no transformation is final. In a certain sense it is even possible that nothing new happens in the world, for everything is but the repetition of the same primordial type".[13]

The salient characteristics of the cyclic view of history are the following. Neither the objects of the external world nor the products of human activity have any intrinsic reality or autonomous validity. History in itself is meaningless. Hence it is periodically abolished or seen as a copy of trans-historical models, or given meta-historical meaning. Things and events derive all their reality and validity from being imitations, participation and repetitions of primordial models and mythical times. Thereby the meaning of time is also abolished to a great extent. Real human time and duration are suspended, all situations remain stationary, and history itself is abolished. The contemporary moment is seen as situated farther from the primordial model and therefore as inferior to it. Every succeeding aeon represents decadence. The countdown of the aeons marks at the same time the approach of a regeneration and of a new cycle. The concept of history in the traditional Indian thinking is also often understood as patterned on a cyclic model. Thus there are four *yuga*, the *satya yuga*, also known as *krta yuga*, which is the Golden Age, and in this age *dharma*, the supreme law governing the world and human life shines forth, while during the *treta yuga,* which follows, *dharma* begins to decline, which is further deteriorated during the *dvapara yuga,* and this is totally destroyed during the *kali yuga,* which is a dark age. The dark age is followed by a cosmic flood, which is known as the *mahapralaya*. What happens next is the emergence of the Golden Age, the *satya yuga*. It may also be noted that the incarnation of God, known as the *avatara,* is also related to this deterioration of *dharma* through the various ages.

This perception of history is also concerned about the periodicity which appears in all human affairs. It sees also cyclic fluctuations and periodic crises in political economy, and corresponding recurrence of times of war and peace, prosperity and poverty, harmony and confrontation. Related to this approach to

---

[12] Mircea Eliaide, *Cosmos and History. The Myth of the Eternal Return* (New York: Harper and Row, 1959), p. 5, 22, 25.

[13] *Ibid.* pp. 88-90.

history, Karl Marx, followed by Hegel, discovered a dialectical movement in history. In this movement of history Marx discerned that a solution of some contradictions generates other contradictions of a higher level of reality with wider range and scope. Through successive solutions of these contradictions, through sharper conflicts and struggles, through more complete overcoming of alienation, history marches forward to fuller socialization. The story of socialization is traced from primitive family groups through tribal communities, the slave state, the feudal setup, capitalism and the bourgeois system towards the awakening of the working class and then to the hoped for socialistic interval and finally the communist society. According to this approach to history progress occurs not in a straight line but along a spiral of struggles against alienating contradictions. As long as alienation lasts, history is insufficiently authentic. Authentic history is created through human actions through the elimination of alienating contradictions which are embodied in the need for profit and exploitation, the need for division of people into classes and the need for private appropriation of socially produced wealth.

This kind of history that comes to birth through this travail of overcoming contradictions and alienation is apparently conceived of as unending. The final stage of this historical process will be one in which men and women will have unhindered possibility of endless creative advance and personal self-realization as free individuals in a community characterized by equality. Marx's idea of the dialectical movement of history is reflected in the following statement: "Men (and women) make their own history, but they do not make just as they please; they do not make it under the circumstances already found, given and transmitted from the past." [14] Humans shape the world and are shaped by it. There is no submission to nature and to the past as in archaic conceptions; nor is there a break with them as in a linear model of history. And the presence of contradictions and alienation are taken seriously. History is a dialectical and spiral process of creative advance.

In the linear model of history there is no repeated return of the same world to the same starting point, the mythical event and the archetype. History is conceived as a creative advance towards a goal. Here history is seen as moving towards fulfillment and will some day come to an end. History has a destiny. Time is not reversible, uniform or static. Rather it is structured, dynamic and it is moving forward towards a goal. It is a one-way reality. The past is not abolished, nor is the future conceived in terms of the past. The distinction and division of time into past, present and future are real. There is a progression of break with the past, through which the present is inaugurated. In this approach real change is admitted and novelty is a characteristic of history. Events are irreversible and they

---

[14] Karl Marx, *The Eighteenth Brumaire of Loius Bonapart (1852)* given in Saul K. Padover, *The Essential Marx* (New York: American Library, 1978), pp. 227-228.

have meaning and value in themselves and in relation to each other, and above all, in relation to the future and the goal of the totality of history. Time is not infinite and history has its own limits. According to Eliade, the Hebrews were the first to make the discovery of a linear understanding of history. It began with Abraham who introduced a history based on the category of faith, thus linking history with a religious experience. For Abraham and for the succeeding generations, faith was the expression of freedom from the natural law of cyclic movement. It was a creative approach to time and history which has God for its source and support. Consequently, the revelation given to Moses takes place in time, in a historical duration, in a limited time and place, which is not reversible. The Hebrew prophets perceived the will of God in the victories and defeats, the triumphs and catastrophes and sufferings of their nation. During the course of history God punished the people for not keeping faith in him, but he also promised and worked out deliverance for them, thus orienting the people towards the future and placing them in a trajectory of hope.

It is out of this linear approach to historical process that there grew up the Messianic expectation. Under the pressure of a history of uncertainty and suffering and supported by the prophetic promise of a future revival, a new interpretation of events began to dawn among the people of Israel. Historical events began to be regarded as part of God's active presence among the people. Thus history was interpreted as a series of theophanies. Each theophany and each event had its intrinsic value because it was God's intervention with a view to the people's final salvation. History was the context for personal encounter between God and the people of Israel. In this manner Israel came to face the challenge of history instead of escaping from it and abolishing it through the possibility of repetitions without end. They accepted history as an ongoing dialogue with Yahweh and regarded every moment as decisive. This Hebrew discovery of time as a one-way reality and of history as the epiphany of God was taken up and further developed by the Christian movement. The early Christian writers opposed the concept of cyclic time and astral influences on human destiny. They traced a straight line for humanity's course from the fall of the humankind to final redemption through Christ. History came to be seen as possessing a unique meaning because at its heart stood the incomparable event of Jesus Christ.

Some observations are in order to understand certain nuances of these and similar approaches to history. Some conceptions of history exclude God from its process, because God is totally transcendent and he is the wholly other. He comes into history as it were from the outside; he breaks into it to judge and save it, but is not the least affected by it. This is the position of traditional classical theologians. Others, chiefly process theologians, refuse to set up a super-terrestrial, supra-natural being called God, a God up there. For them God is in this world; he is in its process, or he is nowhere. He is passionately involved in human history and is deeply affected by it. Without detriment to his divine perfection he can change and receive into himself every moment, all the good that is in history. Our history itself is a history that we make with God and he with us, in total partnership. History in this view is different in its throb and quality from history judged and saved by an immutable and wholly other God. A second observation is about the inclusion or exclusion of nature in the conception of history. Linear history seems to oppose history to nature because nature as such repeats itself and nothing new ever occurs in it, while linear history is marked by ever-increasing newness. Others refuse to follow this approach and speak about the inner and inter-relationship between history and nature insofar as history is organic to nature. History embraces the whole world process, including the realm of nature and its ongoing movement.

Models of History: A Critique

There has been always a Christian claim that every concept of history is not correct, that only the linear model is compatible with the Christian faith and the Christian understanding of reality. As a whole, Christian faith implies a linear conception of time and history. Consequently, it rejects and transforms all repetitive and cyclic models. The Christian approach to history as a process of time guided by God has its basis in the Bible and it is one of the most powerful presentation of the God's dealings with the humankind as an ongoing process with a beginning and an end. Whereas the first statement of the Bible is about a beginning when God created everything (Gen 1:1), the concluding statement in the Bible is about the same God engaged in the creation of a new heaven and a new earth, when he would make his eternal dwelling with the whole humankind (Gen 21:1-4). It is important to observe that through these two statements the biblical authors are trying to place God and history within the largest perspective with its beginning and end as initiated by God. Even the final scene of history is one of God uniting himself with the whole humankind, and not with any particular people chosen by God. So the Bible places things and events within their universal framework. Consequently, the attempt of some Christian theologians to see biblical history and consequently Christian understanding of history in their isolation from other historical happenings and movements is not at all a justified one.

It also is to be emphasized that the cyclic model of history does not seem to be quite so primitive and meaningless and it is not incompatible with Christian faith and thought. The cyclic approach to history is not meant to abolish the dynamism of history. Rather it is a way of living in history which includes nature and relating life to the nature, which constitutes the entire history-making process. We belong to the nature and to the cosmos and our existence is bound up with its ongoing rhythm. We grow and mature through the nature's cycles, and time grows and matures with us as we sleep and wake, work and rest, eat and celebrate life again and again, sing the same songs and repeat the same words of love and affection. In fact, we move forward on nature's cycles of day and night, the cycles of weeks, months and year; the cycles of spring, summer, autumn and winter and during this process we reach the moment of opportunity and the hour of decision. We are all engaged in a cycling process towards distant destinations. At the basis of our entire technological civilization lies the cyclic motion of the wheel, which is repeating the same movement as it moves forward. Hence the wheel is the eternal symbol of cyclic motion of life that was invented by the primitive people at the dawn of civilization as a sign of its yearning for movement towards the future and their goal.

Understood in this manner, every celebration of the Lord's Supper is a proclamation of the death of the Lord until he comes (1 Cor 11:26), and this goes on in a cyclic manner. This celebration, taking place here and now, is at the same time related to the past event of the death of the Lord and also to his future coming. The celebration, as such, is meant to carry human commitment further forward and to bring it to higher levels with wider horizons. Every celebration is intended to be a fresh creation of meaning, a new structuring of time and an intense realization of the kingdom of God which has already arrived. Even the persons, who are committed to the most linear thinking of history, perform a series of repetitive gestures like breathing and walking. They go to their places of work, go back home in the evening, only to repeat the same during the following days and years. Many live between memories and hope, looking back to the promises made and the contracts signed. In fact, for everyone life is a myth of eternal return. The present is always flowing into the past and the future is taking its energy from the present. But there is also a way in which the past flows into the present and into the future at the deeper levels of meaning and consequences. The future remains a future which is incessantly coming into the present to transform it into a fuller and finer tomorrow. The future is the *eschaton,* the final coming of the kingdom of God. This kingdom has already come and it is still coming. Those who believe and love have already passed from death to life. In such a conception of reality neither linear nor cyclic models of history can prove helpful. We need a multi-dialectical conception of time and history which perhaps is yet to be worked out.[15]

History and Mythology

History and mythology are also closely related. Whereas history is the awareness of what happened, mythology is often understood as the effort to understand what has happened through stories and descriptions which may or may not have happened. Myth is often and wrongly defined as "a purely fictitious

---

[15] Cf. Samuel Rayan, *art. cit.* pp. 15-21.

narrative usually involving supernatural persons, actions, or events, and embodying some popular idea concerning natural or historical phenomena".[16] Insofar as one may speak of an emerging consensus, myth may be broadly defined as a narrative (story) concerning fundamental symbols which are constitutive or paradigmatic for human existence. Historians of religion, while often differing on how to interpret any specific myth, tend to agree that all myths, through the use of symbolic language, communicate transcendent meaning within a culture, revealing its cosmic dimensions. Myth is a universal human phenomenon. It attempts to express through symbols the ultimate reality, which transcends both the capacity of discursive reasoning and expression in ordinary human language. Myth in some form appears in almost every culture. It deals with questions of cosmic and human origins, the origins of human institutions, human quest for happiness and its success or failure in finding it, and the end of the world. The principal function of myth is cosmicization, namely, making the world livable and lovable. Its story is timeless and paradigmatic for the present. For this reason the story is often placed either in primordial time or in eschatological time after the present world has come to an end. Since myth has its own importance in the history of all peoples, it is necessary that we give sufficient attention to its inner message. In a certain sense, mythology is the beginning of theology. Through myths people tried to articulate their sense of history and become related to historical developments.

Myth to some extent is an essential part of the patterns of human thought and discourse, which can never be entirely replaced by logical discourse, particularly regarding those questions for which logical discourse fails to render an answer which satisfies the mind. Hence myth can be understood as a symbolic, approximate expression of truth which the human mind cannot perceive sharply and completely but only glimpse vaguely, and therefore cannot adequately or accurately express. Hence myth implies, not falsehood, but truth; not primitive, naïve misunderstanding but an insight more profound than scientific description and logical analysis can ever achieve. The language of myth in this sense is consciously inadequate, being simply the nearest we can come to a formulation of what we see very darkly.

A unique characteristic of Old Testament writers is that they have done their best in making use of mythological stories in narrating the origin of the world and the many events connected with it. The mythological literature of Mesopotamia and Canaan has influenced the language and imagery of the biblical descriptions, such as the creation accounts, the deluge, the condition and fall of the first human couple. But what distinguishes these passages of the Old Testament from ancient mythology is not the patterns of thought and language, which seem in every respect to be the same, but rather the Hebrew idea of God as

---

[16] *Oxford Dictionary*

known through his revelation of himself. This knowledge they themselves attributed to a personal encounter with God. When we compare the thought processes of the Old Testament with the processes of Semitic mythology, we observe that the Old Testament rejects all elements which are out of character with the God whom they knew. But what they knew of God could be expressed only through symbolic form and concrete cosmic event, and the relations of God with the world and with the humankind were perceived and expressed through the same patterns and processes which elsewhere we call mythical.

When we discuss the relation between history and mythology, some tend to understand mythology as the very opposite of history, while others try to see some elements of history in mythological descriptions. It is in this latter sense that Rudolf Bultmann understood mythology, because he maintained that the historical event of Jesus Christ has been transmitted to us mostly in mythological form. But since our present consciousness does not share the mythological worldview of the Greco-Roman mind, it is unable fully to understand the biblical texts and the message behind them. Therefore Bultmann suggested that we should demythologize, that is, interpret these New Testament myths in order to retrieve for us the basic proclamation (*kerygma*) of what God has done in Jesus Christ. Existentialist philosophy, particularly the work of Martin Heidegger, provided Bultmann with the principal question for his interpretation of the New Testament: how does the text challenge the modern reader's self-understanding? The factual history of Jesus of Nazareth's life and death is only essential as the event of God's judgment of the world and in its historical particularities. Important for us is *that* God calls us, through the kegyma of Jesus Christ, to accept that we live by God's grace and find out true human authenticity only in God's love. This *that* of God's call is more important than the *how* of its historical expression. So it is more important to appreciate the eschatological message contained in mythological formulations like Incarnation, sacrificial death, and victory over demonic forces. In spite of Bultmann's hermeneutical initiative which led to a fruitful and sometimes heated debate in all Christian Churches and which showed the need for new ways of biblical interpretation, it must be said that this reduction of the gospel into a mere call for existential decision and the subsequent a-historical approach to Jesus Christ do not seem satisfactory today. Such a timeless kerygma will quickly lose its connection with an always changing consciousness. Bultmann's existential interpretation may be appreciated as an important effort to proclaim the gospel in a particular historical and philosophical context. While this context of the post-war situation in Europe has changed considerably since Bultmann's time, and such a context does not exist in other parts of the world, his hermeneutical insistence that the biblical texts do not just speak for themselves, but rather always call for contextualized interpretation, remains a challenge for all future generations of Christians all over the world.

History and Apocalyptics

The biblical concept of history is also closely related to a unique type of thinking and speculation in Israel and the early Church known as biblical apocalypse, a style of reflection strongly linked to biblical prophecy. The wisdom tradition also influenced the apocalyptic in its growth and development. However closely related prophecy and apocalyptic may be, they are to be distinguished from each other. The prophets, on the whole, declared God's word to their generation, the apocalyptists record revelation said to have been made known by God to some great hero in earlier times and now to be revealed. So also, whereas the prophets see the realization of God's purpose within the historical process, the apocalyptists see that purpose reaching its culmination not within history but above and beyond history in a supramundane realm where God dwells. The apocalypse type of writing, which forms the core of this literature, is a record of divine disclosures made known through the agency of angels, dreams, and visions. These may take different forms, such as an otherworldly journey in which the secrets of the cosmos are made known or a survey of history often leading to an eschatological crisis in which the cosmic powers of evil are destroyed, the cosmos is restored, and Israel is redeemed. During the various stages of the formation of the Old and New Testaments, the biblical writers succeeded in assimilating literary elements and thought patterns borrowed from neighbouring cultures to propound their own message. Wisdom literature of the Old Testament is very much influenced by Mesopotamian and Egyptian wisdom writings. Ezekiel had recourse to Mesopotamian symbolism. The angelology and demonology of Tobit made use of Iranian elements. Apocalyptic was born in an environment where an Iranian and Babylonian syncretism encountered Hellenistic civilization.

It is quite easy to discern the psychological situation in which this literary evolution took place. It is the feverish expectation which characterizes the times of crisis which the post-exilic community of the Jews lived through. The disappointment which followed the return of the first exiles, the political upheavals of the 4th century with their inevitable repercussions on Judaism, aroused feelings of eschatological anguish, which are brought to a climax by the bloody conflict with the totalitarian empire of Antiochus Ephiphanes (170-164 BCE). Neither the legalism bequeathed by Ezra to the Jewish theocracy nor the reflective wisdom of the rising schools of sages, were powerful enough to satisfy this passionate expectation. This is the climate in which the eschatological message was given a new form of expression, that of a supernatural wisdom coming from meditation of the Scriptures revealing the divine secrets to the believers. At the height of the Maccabean crisis, apocalyptic produced its first masterpieces, with Daniel and the most ancient portions of Enoch.

The apocalyptic writers were mainly concerned with the working out of God's plan in history in the perspective of the last judgment and trans-historical eschatology. By letting an ancient seer speak for them, they take their stand in the distant past, thus gaining a vantage point from which they can survey at a glance considerable periods of history. As tracts for the times, apocalypses were written to encourage those who were oppressed and saw little or no hope in terms of either politics or armed might. Their message was that God himself would intervene and reverse the situation in which they found themselves, delivering the godly from the hands of the wicked and establishing his rule for all to see. Sometimes such encouragement was given in the form of discourse in which the revelation of God's sovereignty was disclosed. At other times it took the form of a story or legend concerning the ancient worthy in whose name the book was written. What is characteristic of apocalypse is that for it the whole of history is a unity under the overarching purpose of God. However, history is divided into great epochs that must run their predetermined course. Only then will the end come, and with it the dawning of the messianic kingdom and the age to come when evil will be routed and righteousness established forever. Hence present troubles are birth pangs heralding the end and this is associated with a time of crisis and anguish. Sometimes this is described in terms of political action and military struggle; at other times the conflict assumes cosmic proportions involving mysterious happenings on earth and in the heavens, such as earthquakes, famine, fearful celestial portents, and destruction by fire. In this final battle the powers of evil will be utterly destroyed and God's reign will be finally established. Generally speaking, this coming reign of God is established here on this earth. In some instances it has a temporary duration, and is followed by the age to come. In this new divine order, the end will be as the beginning and paradise will be restored. Dualism is sometimes used to describe the discontinuity between this age and the age to come, but continuity remains. A renewed and restored earth is the scene of God's deliverance. In some of these writings the figures of Messiah and Son of Man, among others, are introduced as agents of the coming reign of God. Probably, these represent two originally distinct strands of eschatological expectation which, in course of time, became intertwined.

Living in Time and Committed to History

After our analysis of the various components of time and history and the various approaches to the understanding of history as well as the related concepts of eternity, mythology and apocalyptic, the important question is about how we have to live in time and become committed to history with the other concepts widening the horizons of our reflection. The real problem related to history is not how we picture time and history to ourselves, whether as linear or as cyclic or as dialectical. The real issue is whether we are prepared to make meaningful history and prevent its actual unmaking and destruction. When we are committed to and involved in the making of history, we shall come to know history's shape and face, and we shall also know who its real enemies are. History does not just happen by the passing of time. Linear time is mechanical time. It marks movement of things and is measured by the tick of circular movements inside a chronometer. By itself such time is not history. Different from it is human time which is time as experienced by humans. An hour by the clock is short when the heart experiences happiness and ecstasy; at the same time, it is too long when the heart's experience is pain and anxiety. The time of crisis and the time of hope have a quality and a depth very different from those of the hours of daily routine. All such moments of experience with human meaning belong within the texture of history. Different from these still is the hour of decision-making, of commitment to painful struggle for a cause for others, of selfless sacrificial love, of fellowship and solidarity. Here mechanical time is taken into the depths of human existence. Thereby time is humanized, historicized, and is given new contents and meaning. Here time begins to be purposeful and forward-looking. Time begins to have a face. It is in and with such moments and actions that history is made. We make history. We make the world and its future through history and thereby we make ourselves. When the others coming to meet us are given a response, when we become partners in life's projects, history is made at levels that are profoundly authentic and human. In fact, history is a matter of authentic relationships which we have to build, cultivate and nurture. Its contents and quality are determined by the kind of relationship we create or fail to create. Wherever injustice is denounced, oppression is resisted, structures of exploitations are dismantled, history is made and God is there. Actions to bring good news to the poor and liberty to captives make history. The making of history and its progress are not to be understood in geometrical terms of the linear and the circular, but in ethical and spiritual terms of the coming of the kingdom of God on the earth and the abundance of its peace among the people. Time and history are the condition of authentic existence.

Globalization as the domination of a uni-polar economic system, facilitating the free movement of capital and trade, would appear to many as a newly invented blessings for the humankind and a new stage of the progress of human history. In reality the relationship that is established through this approach is one of domination-dependence between the rich and the poor countries. It is a combined myth of economic, political and cultural exploitation. The repeated Earth Summits on Sustainable Development from Rio in 1992 to Johannesburg in 2002 have convincingly proved that the ultimate aim of the developed nations is to keep the poor nations subservient to their established life style. These unhealthy trends do not make history, nor do they contribute anything to the progress of history. Rather they unmake history and destroy the foundations on which an authentic history of the humankind at large is to be built up. Plunder and pollution of nature, geared to competitive profit making and consumerism are acts which unmake history. History is unmade by oppression and injustice and the violation of the rights of men and women. Colonialism in the past was the unmaking of history. Fortunately, it has come to an end. But new forms of colonialism are in the offing. It takes time for the poor nations to realize that their history will be adulterated through these new forms of exploitation.

By contrast, history will be made and re-made by the people who will wake up to reality and struggle for freedom and justice for the oppressed and the exploited. It is a history enacted and it is being enacted in the struggle of the people of South Africa against apartheid and terrorism, in the struggle of the blacks for freedom in the United States, in the struggle of the *dalits* in India against untouchability, caste system, landlessness and feudal capitalism. There are defeats and victories in that process, there are reversals and hopes associated with these struggles. There are times of celebrations and mourning. The question is not whether this history is understood as linear or cyclical or dialectical. The geometrical vocabulary of linear and circular, or vertical and horizontal in theology and life can be a diversionary tactic to distract us from the tasks of the present and the demands of the *eschaton* which has already arrived with the coming of the kingdom of God and which we must make arrive more and more in the ongoing process of history.

The Bible traces the meaning of history not in terms of linear and cyclical, but in terms of justice and freedom through concrete struggles. But it is possible to dehistoricize the Bible and reduce its historical message to some general spiritual principles with no solid principles to grapple with the hard realities of our earthly existence. It has been possible to dehistoricize and eternalize Christ, a Christ who was very much God. Orthodox theology does not deny the historical humanity of Christ; it simply disregards it and ignores it. Orthodox theology is concerned with Christ's eternal human nature, but not with the contingent event of Christ in the world, nor with the fact that Christ belongs totally to history. We have to take the 'now' of Christ seriously. This 'now' is the hour of justice and life which is come into history. It is a summons to transform the earth and make authentic human history happen. Time and history are ethical and ontological. They can be shown and known only in an ethical resolution. History is made of the outcry of all the oppressed and the exploited. It is in that it consists and it is in that bears fruits.

Transcending Time and open to Eternity

Christian existence is characterized by a certain prophetic impatience for the simple reason that it has to combine time and eternity in one embrace. As such, it is easier to accept one and reject the other; but the challenge and beauty of life consist in the fact that it can and should accept both time and eternity, the power for which comes from the Christ Event itself. In Christ time and eternity met and penetrated each other, one giving meaning to the other. It is now the task of all Christians to face the challenge and accept the promise offered by this event. This they have to do through their Christian reflection and through the totality of their life with its success and failures, with its joy and suffering, and also with its promises and challenges. It is neither escapism from time nor an exclusive identification with time; rather it is controlled by a principle of involvement and transcendence.

The central events described in the Bible, both in the Old and the New Testaments, are at the same time events rooted in time and history as well as metaphors and parables transcending history and reaching out to eternity. The call of Abraham, the liberation of Israel from Egypt, the making of the covenant, the wandering of Israel in the wilderness, the division of the kingdom into two after Solomon, the overthrow of the Northern Kingdom, the Babylonian captivity and the restoration from the exile are all events which continue to play their related and respective roles in the history of all peoples. The important point is that people should have their ability to read the meaning of their own history within the context of the message of these events. Though the Israelites were not culturally and academically so advanced as the Canaanites and many of their neighbouring peoples, such as in Egypt and Babylon, the theological and religious insights the Hebrew writers have bequeathed to their future generations are far advanced and fascinating, and they can still inspire the present and future generations with their profound religious sense. What science and technology have provided the humankind during the past many centuries through their significant contributions could be said to be marvellous. But what the Israelite religion has transmitted to humanity in the distant past through its profound insight into its God-experience could be considered as something unparalleled in the history of religion.

The human condition of being in time with a role to play in history, thereby making meaning for one's own life and for the lives of others receives another equally important consideration insofar as all are invited to transcend the parameters of time and history and open themselves to the challenge of eternity which belong to it as their eschatological goal. As spirited matter, humans belong to the realm of matter and spirit and it is important for all to affirm the demands of both these realms of being in their everyday life. We have traces of this line of thinking in the Old Testament in the directives given about the observance of the Sabbath, the sabbatical year and the celebration of the Jubilee Year. These celebrations were meant also to train the Israelites to develop a culture of living in this world and transcending this world, affirming this world and denying this world and thereby transcending the realities of this world. The inner meaning of these directives was to show the people that their existence and activities in this world are not their ultimate goal of life. This awareness they were exhorted to maintain periodically, either as a weekly phenomenon in the observance of the Sabbath, or as a periodic remembrance during the celebration of the sabbatical year and the Jubilee Year.

The same could be said about the New Testament and its unique contribution in the realm of Christ experience which was considered as the greatest treasure of the early Church. Writing to the Romans about what God has done to the humankind through Christ, Paul refers to the revelation of God's plans in and through Jesus Christ as an eternal *now*. "Precisely now[17] the righteousness of God has been revealed apart from the Law, and it is attested by the Law and Prophets" (Rom 3:21). Paul knew very well that the great events related to the public ministry, passion, death and resurrection of Christ took place in the distant past away in Jerusalem. But those historical limitations have nothing to do with the eternal presence of the Christ Event through its saving and redeeming dimensions. Here the specifications of time and space as well as their historical vicissitudes have been transcended and all can now look up to the eternal and time-transcending message. The same transcending message is found also in Paul's powerful testimony about the celebration of the Lord's Supper. Paul writes to the Corinthians: "As often as you eat this bread and drink the cup, you proclaim the Lord's death until he comes" (1 Cor 11:26). The celebration of the Lord's Supper is the meeting point of the past, present and the future in a convergent point of time, where the past becomes present and points to the future. It is an act of the community of believers through which its members try to experience the power of the past which empowers the present and prepares them for the future. It is a proclamation of what God has done in the past with its challenge for the present and its promise for the future.

The author of the book of Revelation presented Christ as seated on the throne and declaring: "I am the Alpha and the Omega, the beginning and the end" (Rev 21:6). Jesus Christ is the same yesterday and today and forever (Heb 13:8), wrote the author of the letter to the Hebrews. The one who was in the beginning and who began the historical process is also the one who concludes it and brings it to fulfillment. It was the privilege and task of humanity and the entire cosmos to be included in this historical process through an active and creative participation, and God brings it to completion at the fullness of time when he would bring all things to Christ as the head of the creation and the conclusion of the historical process (Eph 1:10). Even as the humankind is engaged in building up its own secular city with its gigantic political and economic plans, God is guiding the entire historical process towards its eschatological realization when God would become all in all (*ta panta en pasin*) (1 Cor 15:28). God is the originator of time; he is also the author of history. As one who transcends time and history, he

---

[17] The Greek expression is an emphatic *nuni*, which means precisely at this moment. Paul refers to the past Christ Event as something taking place now, precisely at the moment of his writing.

assimilates time and history into himself through the final union of all things into the eternal now. Eternity is both that which gives rise to time and that from which time ceaselessly flows, and it is also that which bestows upon time its meaning and teleology.

II

WORLD HISTORY AND SALVATION HISTORY

Until the dawn of the Age of Reason a dual conception of history, which had gradually been evolving since the early Middle Ages, was the universally accepted way in which Christendom regarded the past. It is implicit in the eighteenth-century phrase, *history sacred and profane*. Accordingly, the total of human historical knowledge could be divided into two quite distinct types, differing on account of the disparate sources from which they came. Sacred history was the history of the world as it was divinely and therefore without any error disclosed in the Bible. This history was complete and superior in itself not only for all its past since the creation of the world, but also for all its future until its consummation in the Last Judgment. This sacred history was also known as salvation history, meaning thereby that it was necessary to be included in this sacred history if humans wanted to arrive at salvation in the next life. There was no choice possible. Until the final disintegration of the medieval world-view in the eighteenth century, world history, also known as profane history, had to be fitted into the periphery of this sacred history of the Bible, as it had been since the time of Orosius in the early fifth century CE.[1] This conception of sacred history, derived from the infallible teaching of the Bible, and supplying the framework into which all other histories had to be somehow accommodated, survived among the Christians until after the close of the Age of Reason. Profane[2] history or world history, as contrasted with this sacred history or salvation history, was purely a human enterprise which has no goal and no meaning. There was therefore an absolute qualitative difference between sacred and profane history. Everything except the sacred history was secondary, a marginal reality. Hence world history was held in low esteem by many Christian theologians.[3]

It is this dichotomic approach to history as sacred and profane that has prevailed in Christian thinking till very recent times. The history of the world, the history of other world religions, political histories were all seen as not related to salvation history and they only served as the framework and the matrix within which the sacred history took place and this sacred history

---

[1] Augustine had commissioned his scholarly researcher, Orosius, to write a more orderly complement to his own discursive *De Civitate Dei*.

[2] The adjective 'profane' is derived from the Latin *profanes*, which literally meant 'before the temple', i.e. 'non-sacred', unconsecrated', 'secular'.

[3] Cf. Alan Richardson, *History Sacred and Profane* (London: SCM Press, 1964) pp. 23-26.

was identified with the biblical revelation. But a real change has taken place in our times with the emergence of what we may call a process of secularization. In fact, the world of today has become very much secular, and it would appear that the process is by no means over yet. Secular thinking is the keynote of contemporary philosophical, scientific and theological thinking. As a result, the trend in the various areas of human reflection is to underline the secular dimension of human life and human history. This universal secularity challenges the faith of millions of people and they are faced with the question as to what their attitude to secularity should be. It could happen that faith would try to ignore the acuteness of the situation and simply hammer away behind locked doors at its customary practices in theology and piety, as though there had been no worthwhile issue, and therefore there is no need to understand and answer the challenges of the ever changing times. A faith that is unhistorical is not likely to feel itself threatened. It can go on talking with extraordinary superiority about God and the world. But it lacks urgency and a taste of reality. Some would see this whole situation as a denial of the sacred, while others see it as the sign of an ushering in of a complementary approach in human thinking, where the natural and the supernatural, the this-worldly and the other-worldly, the sacred and the secular have their respective roles to play. It is also related to the dynamics of a theocentric and anthropocentric approach, where both the divine and the human are to be seen in complementary dimensions, enriching each other and not opposed to each other. The very approach to the Bible as the Word of God in human language, which has inaugurated the scientific study of the Bible towards the end of the 19th century and during the 20th century was an affirmation of the complementary dimension of the sacred as associated with salvation and the secular or the so-called profane. Thereby a new understanding of history and a new approach to the action of God in history have also emerged.

Salvation History within World History

When Christian thinkers developed the concept of a linear understanding of history as the unique contribution of the Old and New Testaments within the larger framework of cyclic and circular approach to history, there grew up a tendency to consider the history of Israel and the history of the Christian movement as an ongoing process of salvation history, starting with the creation and the call of Abraham and reaching its goal and realization in the Christ Event, from where the salvation history moves forward in the history of the Christian movement in ever-widening dimensions till it reaches its consummation in the second coming of Christ. Hence the first eleven chapters of the Book of Genesis were understood as the stage of world history, while from Genesis chapter twelve onwards there is the inauguration of the salvation history with the call of Abraham which is later focused on the history of Israel. This history underwent many vicissitudes until in a unique figure of Messianic expectation the whole history of salvation was concentrated. In Jesus of Nazareth this Messianic hope of salvation was realized and from him onwards the salvation history took new dimensions, inviting people to join this mainstream of salvation. Accordingly, it was maintained that the Church, to which the work of salvation is entrusted, has to bring in as many people as possible so that they can also come out of the realm of world history and belong to the history of salvation. Here lies the meaning of mission and evangelization as well as the whole meaning of the ministry of the Church in the world.

Thus O. Cullmann made a conscious and consistent effort to see the Christ Event as constituting the middle of time through his work published in German in 1946 under the title *Christus und die Zeit* and translated into English as *Christ and Time* in 1951. He wrote: "In Christ time has reached its mid-point, and at the same time the moment has reached in which this is preached to men (and women), so that with the establishment of the division of time, they are able to believe in it and in this faith to understand time in a Christian way, that is taking Christ as the Centre"[4] In his efforts to explain the unique characteristics of the theology of Luke, Hans Conzelmann also tried to understand the ministry of Jesus of Nazareth as the 'Centre of Time', which is preceded by the history of Israel and is followed by the period since the ascension of Christ, which is the period of the Church. The German edition, *Die Mitte der Zeit,* was published in 1953 and its English translation came out in 1960 as *Theology of Luke*. Around the middle of the 20th century this approach to biblical theology and time was a standard in theological writings.[5]

Though it was a fascinating idea to evaluate history during those years for all theologians, when Western theologians were supposed to have the right to say the last word about anything theological and biblical, now theologians and exegetes in general are not all happy with this approach to the Christian understanding of history. This is not to deny the importance of the Christ Event in history nor somehow to relativize the role of Christ in salvation history taken as a whole, a fear that is being expressed again and again in the documents of the Church. More important for us is to understand God as guiding the entire historical process within which we have to see and understand the person of Christ and his redemptive mission. The salient perspectives of God's involvement in the history of Israel and of the early Church are mainly faith articulations of Israel and the early Church. We must respect their commitment to their faith, with which they responded to

---

[4] Oscar Cullmann *Christ and Time*: *The Primitive Christian Conception of Time and History* (Translated by Floyd V. Filson) (London: SCM Press Ltd, 1951) p. 93.

[5] Cf. Neal M. Flanagan, *Salvation History: An Introduction to Biblical Theology* (New York: Sheed and Ward, 1964).

God's revelation. But it is not correct to make these faith expressions as applicable to all humans and also to apply this approach as a criterion for evaluating all events in the world history.

The fact that this assumption of Christian theologians was not questioned in the past is not a justification for the contemporary academic world to continue using it during these changed times in a pluralistic culture like ours. What we can say is that in this exercise of superiority complex the Christians were following a kind of Constantine syndrome, which started in the fourth century of the Common Era and which later on was revived during the time of the Crusades and after the 14th century through the colonialism organized from the Christian West with its military and missionary power trying to conquer the whole world. This questionable programme of the conquest of the world was based on two major assumptions: One, that Christianity is the only true religion and that all other religions are false. Again there were specifications. Only the Roman Catholic Church is the true Church and all other Christians were separated brethren. The second assumption was that earthly life was only a preparation for the life after death. Salvation of the soul was the main agenda of Christian mission.

As Dietrich Bonhoeffer, one of the most challenging theologians of 20th century, has affirmed, our world is a world "come of age". The world has grown into maturity. As a result, some of the unhealthy assumptions and uncritical approaches to reality prevailing among Christians have been willingly given up without anybody questioning them or fighting for them. Theologians all over the world started looking at the world and history through new eyes. They have begun to see that there is only one God and one human community, and consequently there is only one history with many dimensions. Ethnic, social, cultural and political events are all part of this history that was guided by the same God. According to Gustavo Gutierrez, there are no two histories, one profane and one sacred, juxtaposed or closely linked. Rather there is only one human history and one human destiny. The historical destiny of humanity must be placed definitively in the salvific horizon. Only thus will its true dimensions emerge and its deepest meaning be apparent. It seems, however, that contemporary theology has not yet furnished the categories which would allow us to think through and express adequately this unified approach to history.[6]

Holistic Understanding of Salvation History

A new humanism is on the rise, and accordingly a new approach human life is also seen as a unified whole. Moreover, salvation is understood as embracing the human life taken as a whole. An awareness of selfhood, a

---

[6] Cf. Gustavo Gutierrez, *A Theology of Liberation* (London: SCM Press, 1974), p. 153,

search for purpose in history, and a yearning for new forms of community are the characteristics of the new humanism that is gradually evolving all over the world. This phenomenon is found in all religions. Secular and religious movements are bearers of this new humanism. The ultimate goal of all this process is humanization and this the new name for salvation in its broadest sense. Humanization means the process through which humans are rendered authentic and integrated. Humanization means the process through which humans are enabled to live in dignity as God's children. Humanization means the destruction of all structures of sin, whether social, cultural, religious or even political. Humanization affirms that life here on earth is equally meaningful and relevant as life after death. Humanization means that the whole humankind has a right to enjoy the good things of this world, and the unfortunate division of the humankind into 'haves' and 'have-nots' is unjustified, with 20% of the world population enjoying 80% of the resources of the earth and 80% of the world population constrained to live with the remaining 20% of such resources. Humanization means the eradication of all oppressive structures whether they belong to the old colonialism or the new forms of colonialism coming under the label of globalization.

In fact, what we find in the Old and New Testaments are attempts at seeing God entering into human history and engaged in accomplishing the holistic humanization of the entire humankind. The entire Bible is about a God who creates and acts, a God who is continually involved in the history of humankind. Though the first impression we get about Israel is that it was a community selected from among the nations in order to live in isolation, several writers of the Old Testament are bold enough to articulate the universal and pluralistic background of Israel and their task of being an open community. Thus we have the Elohistic tradition introducing the call of Abraham as God's definitive step to bless all the families of the earth, insofar as Abraham represents the ideal person who commits himself to God and to his saving plans. Abraham is therefore more a paradigm than a particular person, more a parable than an individualized one (Gen 12:1-3). Prophet Ezekiel wrote to the Israelites: "Your origin and your birth were in the land of the Canaanites; your father was an Amorite, and your mother a Hittite" (Ez 16:3). So also Amos spoke to Israel: "Are you not like the Ethiopians to me, O people of Israel? Did I not bring Israel up from the land of Egypt, and Philistines from Caphtor and the Arameans from Kir?" (Am 9:7). All what we find in the Old Testament under the guise of the election of Israel, the divine protection given to them, Israel's hatred towards the nations and the holy wars Israel waged against the nations are the creations of some specific theological traditions behind the Old Testament, and there is a constant effort made by other writers of the Old Testament to emphasize the universal dimensions of God's involvement in Israel's history.

Israel Encountering God in the World History

The Bible also with two detailed narratives about the creation of the world in the Priestly (Gen 1:1-2:4a) and the Yahwist (Gen 2:4b-25) traditions. In both these narratives humankind is the focus of the creation, either as the climax of God's creative act insofar as the men and women are created in God's image and likeness and are given the task of being the steward of the creation (Gen 1:26-31) or as the centre of a beautiful and idyllic garden where God created them and gave them a share in God's own life through the divine breath (Gen 2:7) and invited them to be creative and stewarding in the task entrusted to them (Gen 2:15). But this lofty picture of humankind is reversed through the symbolic story of the fall of the humankind (Gen 3:1-24). This is followed by several kerygmatic stories about the power of sin as to Abel and Cain and his descendants (Gen 4:1-26), about the total corruption of humankind which necessitated the punishment of humankind through the flood (Gen 6:9:17), about the unholy attitude of Ham towards his own father, Noah (Gen 9: 18-27) and lastly about the pride and presumption of humankind which tried to safeguard its own future without any recourse to the assistance of God, with its projected construction of a tower with its top in heavens, an attempt that was defeated by God himself through the confusion of their language (Gen 11:1-9). The entire narrative in these chapters of Genesis has the theme of God creating the world and humankind through his goodness, while humans were not responding to this divine act of love and care through the misuse of their freedom. This theme is presented through various stories about the ascending power of sin and the growing separation of humankind from God, on the one hand, and the punishing, purifying and supporting hand of God, on the other hand.[7] Though we must respect the historical background of these stories, through his Encyclical *Humani Generis* Pope Pius XII has clearly instructed the members of the Church that they should not look for the kind of modern history in these early chapters of Genesis, known as the Primeval History.[8] The mistake in the past had been in taking all these stories as if they had happened the way they are narrated regarding the creation and the fall. The prevailing 'Fall-Redemption' theology and many of its consequences have their background and support in this Primeval History. If we closely analyse these chapters, it becomes clear that the main purpose of these stories is not only to highlight the origin of everything from God but also to theologically establish the reason why God started with a new and unusual beginning with the call of Abraham and the story of the Patriarchs. The basic rationale which links these two major facts lies in the origin of sin and evil in the humankind, in such a way that God proceeded to take some new steps to

---

[7] Cf. G. von Rad, *Genesis* (London: SCM Press, 1961) pp. 148-153.

[8] Cf. J. Dupuis, *The Christian Faith* (Bangalore: Theological Publications in India, 1996) pp.109-110.

guide the humankind to its ultimate goal. So we have to understand the various stories in the Primeval History more as symbolic narratives with their inner message, all of them leading to the significant event of God calling Abraham for the new task he had to play for the history of humankind. In other words, the Old Testament is dealing with these issues within the general framework of world history.

The narratives about the Patriarchs are placed soon after the Primeval History precisely to show that only a humankind ready to obey God can have a future of its own. Thus the stories of Abraham, Isaac, Jacob and Joseph are presented in an entirely new perspective of obedience to and trust in God. Although the Patriarchal narratives (Gen 12-50) have more historical basis than the Primeval History, here again we have to admit the fact that they are more edifying and haggadic stories than real history. Old Testament scholars admit that there is a historical basis for the various patriarchal narratives, although we cannot specify the details. These stories are filled with suspense because of the great display of divine promises and fulfillment associated with them. This expansion of the patriarchal stories into such a surcharged narrative is the product of long work at collecting and even more of superior art in theological composition. The introductory story of Abraham's departure from his own homeland and his later history together constitute a paradigmatic test of faith and its response, because he had to start out in complete uncertainty, to learn at his destination that precisely this way into uncertainty was the movement toward a great and saving God. The complex stories about the patriarchs are narrated in such a way that they left behind a message about how humans have to stand before God in humility and hope. This is symbolized in the last words of Joseph to his brothers, who hated him and ill-treated him: "Even though you intended to do harm to me, God intended it for good, in order to preserve a numerous people, as he is doing today" (Gen 50: 20). The God of Israel guided his people within the framework of world history in order to reveal that his plans are ultimately universal. Hence we read about the ultimate purpose of the call of Abraham as God's plans to bless all families of the earth (Gen 12:1-3).

Although the book of Genesis begins with the story of the creation of the whole universe, thereby preparing the larger background for the history of Israel, it is the considered view of Old Testament scholars that the basic and central story of the Old Testament is the narrative of the exodus from Egypt and the many events related to this primordial event. Here we encounter a God entering into the heart of human history with a definite plan about Israel. Though it is the story of the God of Israel getting involved in the destiny of a particular people, the story is to be understood also as a paradigm and as a pattern of how God is concerned about all humans and how he wants to liberate the oppressed and the exploited wherever and whenever it happens in the course of history. Even the detailed story of the patriarchs in the book of Genesis is arranged in such a way that this major story of Israel appears as a natural sequence to the story of the patriarchs. Hence the prologue to the central story of the Old Testament is God speaking to Moses from the burning bush: "I have observed the misery of my people who are in Egypt. I have heard their cry on account of their taskmasters. Yes, I know their sufferings. And I have come down to deliver them from the Egyptians, and to bring them up out of that land to a good and broad land, a land flowing with milk and honey, to the country of the Canaanites, the Hitttites, the Amorites, the Perizzites, the Hivites and the Jebusites. The cry of the Israelites has now come to me, I have also seen how the Egyptians oppress them. So come, I will send you to Pharaoh to bring my people, the Israelites, out of Egypt" (Ex 3: 7-10). It is this stirring historical drama that is unfolded in the book of Exodus. The protagonist is Israel's God, who intervenes on behalf of a helpless band of slaves. The plot, developed through a succession of suspense-filled episodes, is God's contest against the Egyptian Pharaoh, the mightiest emperor of the day. The denouement comes when, in the nick of time, Israel's pursuers are swallowed up in the waters of the Sea of Reeds. The leading theme of the drama is the action and triumph of God over human malice.

From the Egyptian point of view the exodus was just a marginal political event: the liberation of a band of slaves from the yoke of Pharaoh with no political consequence. That was all its public meaning. In that sense it can be viewed and compared with similar political events in the lives of other peoples. But to Israel the exodus was an event with a divine purpose and plan. What happened to them was God's redemption of his people, not just their liberation from political servitude. The exodus was an act of God and it was a sign of his loving presence in the midst of the people. Therefore the story of the exodus deals with history on a different plane from that on which much of our history is usually written and studied today. No external historical study can demonstrate that the exodus was an act of God; it was politically an insignificant event. But to Israel this political event was the medium through which God's presence among the Israelites and his purpose about them were disclosed. God's revelation to Israel did not come like a bolt from the blue; it came through the crises of a divine dimension of meaning. The general public was unaware of the whole thing. For Israel, it was full of meaning, both for them and for their future. For the Hebrew writers to write history was to narrate these mighty acts of God.

What is significant about this history of Israel is the fact of God encountering Moses and making him the instrument in his hands for executing God's plans about Israel. God is fully aware of the problem and Moses also is aware of it because he had run away from Egypt after an indignant outburst of anger against an Egyptian slave-driver. In human reckoning Moses was a murderer, a sinner. But God has taken a final decision about him and Moses is to be there to take charge of God's plans. God speaks a language of concern: "I have *seen*...I have *heard*.... I *know*.... I have *come down* to deliver them" (Ex 3:7-11). Moses is also thereby challenged to feel with God and thereby get ready for involvement and action. His encounter with God sharpened his sense of individuality, which was already there when he came to the rescue of a poor Hebrew (Ex 2:11-12), and it made him more acutely conscious of the demands of the historical situation. In the 'I and Thou' dialogue Moses was given a task and he was summoned to take his part in a historical drama. Moses hesitated because of his own limitations and the seriousness of the mission entrusted to him. He was inclined to stay on the comfortable sidelines of history, watching it from a distance. But God had chosen him to be his instrument for the realization of his plans.

In this context it is very useful to reflect on the very revelation of the divine name 'Yahweh' made to Moses on mount Sinai, through which God wanted to identify himself as different from all other gods. In Hebraic thought it was believed that any name is filled with a mysterious power and significance, for the name represents the innermost self or identity of a person. In the exodus story we come to one of the most cryptic passages in the Old Testament. When Moses asked God for his name, he answered Moses: "I am who I am" or "I will be what I will be" (Ex 3:14). He further said: "Thus you shall say to the Israelites: 'I AM has sent me to you'. In Ex 3:15 God continues: "YHWH, the God of your ancestors, the God of Abraham, the God of Isaac, and God of Jacob, has sent me to you': This is my name forever; and this is my title for all generations". YHWH,[9] technically known as the tetragrammaton, is most probably the third person rendering of the first person YHYH. As we reflect on the meaning of this name of God, it is important that we understand this name not in the abstract, but as closely related to his involvement and action in the ongoing developments of the history of Israel. Hence the context of this revelation of the divine name is very important. Though God was addressed through several other names, such as El Shaddai, El Elyon, it was to Moses on Mount Sinai that the official name of God as Yahweh was first of all revealed (Ex 3:14). But the Yahwist tradition, with its own theological preoccupation, maintains that the God of Israel was always known as Yahweh (Gen 4:26).

---

[9] In the Old Testament period Hebrew language was written only with consonants; vowels were not added until the early Christian era, when Hebrew was no longer a living language. It is now accepted that the original pronunciation of the Hebrew YHWH was *Yahweh*. But because of the holy aspect of this name, it was withdrawn from ordinary speech after the exile and the substitute Hebrew ADONAI (Lord) was introduced. The still prevailing pronunciation *Jehovah* is the result of an erroneous combination of the consonants of YHWH with the vowels of ADONAI, added to it during the Christian times.

The Hebrew etymology of this divine name 'Yahweh' is a disputed one among biblical scholars. The LXX rendered it as "I am who I am" (*ego eimi ho on)*, the emphasis here being on God's changeless essence and being, that is, he is the God who eternally is, who is not affected by the flux and flow of time. The ancient Greeks, who struggled philosophically with the problem of the changing and the changeless, would have favoured such a view. But in Israel's faith the emphasis is upon divine activity. Just as persons disclose themselves to others through their words and deeds, so also God reveals himself by what he does. There is general agreement among biblical scholars that the name 'Yahweh' is derived from the archaic form of the verb *to be (hawah)*. The Hebrew verb *to be* has a dynamic meaning that cannot be rendered by the English verb *to be*. There are other etymologies also proposed. W.F. Albright has interpreted the name as derived from the causative form of the verb *to be* and proposes that Yahweh is only the first word of the entire name *yahweh aser yihweh*, translated as "He brings into being whatever comes to being". The name therefore designates God as one who acts and gets involved in human history.[10] The most concrete form of God's involvement in history was the deliverance of Israel from Egypt and the making of the covenant on mount Sinai. It is within the context of God active in the history of Israel that he was revealed and hence this name stands for his dynamic presence with the people of Israel. God reveals himself as a force in the future of the people and not as an abstract being separated from history. According to another hypothesis, Yahweh was formerly the mountain god of Kenites, a clan of the Midianites, and Moses was initiated into the Yahweh cult through his marriage to the daughter of Jethro, the priest of Midian. It was while Moses was tending Jethro's flocks in the Midianite territory that he received a revelation from Yahweh. But the significant point here is not where the name came from, or even what its literal meaning could be. Rather, the important issue is what the name stood for in the history of Israel from the time of Moses onwards. The Israelites knew and worshiped Yahweh as the one who had heard their cry of their oppression, who had graciously intervened on their behalf, and who had led them toward a future full of promise. In Israel's experience, as interpreted by Moses, the name 'Yahweh' had only one meaning: "I am Yahweh who brought you up out of the land of Egypt".[11]

The concrete expression of the abiding presence of Yahweh among the Israelites was the making of the covenant on mount Sinai, through which God entered into a permanent relationship with Israel, and the tangible sign

---

[10] Cf. W.F. Albright, *From Stone Age to Christianity* (New York: Doubleday Anchor Books, 1957) pp.15-18; 259-272.

[11] Cf. B.W. Anderson, *Understanding the Old Testament* (Englewood Cliffs: Prentice-Hall, 1957) pp. 36-37.

of this relationship was the giving of the Torah that was supposed to guide the religious and social life of the people. As a covenant community, Israel was expected to become a kingdom of priests and a holy nation (Ex 19:4-6), which was more a task than a privilege. The making of the covenant between Yahweh and Israel in Exodus 24:1-18 is a dramatic illustration of the personal relationship that was established between God and Israel through that event. G. E. Mendenhall has shown that the external form of the covenant on Sinai resembles the suzerainty treaty imposed upon a vassal king and it is well illustrated in the Hittite treaties contracted during the 14th and 13th centuries BCE. Through the Sinai covenant Yahweh imposed certain religious and social obligations upon Israel and in return he promised to be their God, to assist them and to deliver them in their trials and troubles. The Israelites accepted the obligations, the most important of which was to worship no other god but Yahweh. If they were to become unfaithful, Yahweh would withdraw his favour. In virtue of the covenant the Israelites could appeal to Yahweh's affection and protection and Yahweh in turn demanded a corresponding affection and loyalty from Israel. It was a meeting of persons in the 'I-Thou' context. Through this event the history of Israel was once again sanctified and all events, religious, social and political, that were to happen in their history received a new meaning and a theological significance.

The long history of Israel is the interplay of the demands of a personal relationship between Yahweh and Israel and the poor response Israel gave to Yahweh. Instead of being a witnessing community among the nations, manifesting through their life that they were a wise nation and a discerning people (Deut 4:5-8), Israelites took upon themselves a struggle to establish themselves as superior to all others and they waged wars against others, naming them 'holy wars' which was more a psychological technique to justify their own selfish actions of cruelty and revenge. Yahweh's efforts to guide the people through the judges, through the kings and later on through the prophets did not bear much fruit. The entire question was one of Israel not accepting God's grace as grace but appropriating it as their right and privilege. As the spokespersons of Yahweh, the prophets had a very demanding task to make God's purpose and plans about Israel clear to each generation. Yahweh's commitment to history was final and absolute and hence it was always a question of finding new ways of realizing his plans about humankind. While some prophets spoke about the punishment that was to be meted out to Israel in view of purifying them, others spoke a language of promise and restoration to give them hope and courage. Thus Jeremiah spoke about the New Covenant which would be established by God in the future (Jer 31:31-34) and Ezekiel referred to the purification of Israel and the granting of the Spirit as well as the giving of a new heart to them (Ezek 11:17-20; 36:22-28). The destruction of the Northern Kingdom in BCE 721 and the captivity in Babylon that started in BCE in 587, to which the people of the Southern Kingdom were subjected, became clear proof of God's negative dealings with his chosen people and they constituted a warning and a turning point in the understanding of God's presence and action in history. The Babylonian captivity was a period of intense reflection and meditation for those who had a sense of history and the result of this reflection and meditation is articulated in many books of the Old Testament. The people were exhorted to remember the past as part of renewing their present and preparing themselves to meet the future.

As a result of these developments prophetism in Israel gradually gave way to eschatology and apocalyptism, through which the people who returned from Babylon began to turn their attention from the historical to other-worldly expectations. Eschatology is part of historical thinking and it emphasizes the fulfillment dimension of historical process. In post-exilic Judaism eschatological expectations took several directions, such as political and apocalyptic. Basic to the eschatological thinking in Judaism was a convergence of pessimism and hope, pessimism as a result of the bitter experiences of the destruction of Jerusalem and the captivity, and hope based on the promises God made to Israel from the time of the patriarchs onwards. Consequently, there arose several descriptions of the future. While Proto-Isaiah had spoken about an Emmanuel (Is 7:14) who would restore the blessed times of the Southern Kingdom, Deutero-Isaiah articulated his vision about the future restoration as realized through a suffering servant of the Lord (Is 52:13-53:12) and Trito-Isaiah narrated the future as blessed by the arrival of the one who was anointed by the Spirit of God (Is 61:1-11). The underlying thought in these and similar descriptions is the firm conviction the people had about the need of God's special intervention for the restoration of his people. God cannot stand outside of history because he is the Lord of history and its destiny.

The Sacred and the Secular in the New Testament

It is interesting to find that in the Christmas narrative of the Gospel of Luke the scene opens in the royal palace of Caesar Augustus in Rome, where the emperor orders a census of his *oikoumene* to be taken. From Rome it moves to Syria where the Roman governor Quirinius proceeds to implement the imperial command. Accordingly, a young couple began to travel all the way from Nazareth in Galilee to Bethlehem of Judah where their child was to be born (Lk 2:1-7). Through this description Luke is trying to show the secular and worldly dimensions of the birth of Christ. Again, the beginning of the public ministry of Jesus opens with a description of its political and historical landscape in Rome, around Palestine and in Jerusalem itself (Lk 3:1-2). It goes to the credit of Luke, the great theological historian of the New Testament, who could relate the sacred events of Christian origins to the secular events of the days of King Herod (Lk 1:5), Emperor

Augustus and Governor Quirinius (Lk 2:1-3), as well as to Emperor Tiberius, Governor Pontius Pilate, Herod the ruler of Galilee, Philip the ruler of Ituraea and Trachonitis and Lysanias the ruler of Abilene (Lk 3:1-2). What Jesus of Nazareth did was not an isolated exercise of his projects and plans. It takes the dimensions of the Roman Empire, the *oikoumene* of the then known world. As Paul said in one of his discourses, the Christ event did not happen in some dark corner (Acts 26:26) that nobody knew about; rather it was a public event known to all.

All the Gospels try to explain how through his ministry Jesus continued to be the dynamic presence of God in history. John has articulated this conviction through his very bold statement about the Word, which was with God in the beginning, becoming flesh and dwelling among humans (Jn 1:1-14). Mathew takes care to confirm his first statement about the Emmanuel – God with us – in 1.23 through two other further statements about the continued presence of Christ in the community of his disciples, firstly, in the central part of his Gospel (Mt 18:20) with his promise of presence where two or three are gathered in his name and later on as the conclusion of the Gospel in 28:20, where he declares: "I am with you till the end of the age". Hence the last statement of Mathew is not about the ascension of the risen Jesus, but rather about his continued presence and action till the end of the historical process. Through this new assurance the eschatological expectations of Judaism were once again revised and a new awareness of God's presence in history was confirmed and guaranteed.

Some would argue from these reflections that what Jesus did and what he promised were aspects of a spiritual salvation which was inaugurated by him. It is precisely here that we have to reflect on the earthly and this-worldly understanding of salvation history in the preaching of Jesus. What Jesus brought with his ministry is the inauguration of the kingdom of God. Starting with the first beatitude "Blessed are the poor in spirit, for theirs is the kingdom of heaven", Christian tradition has a vitiated history of understanding the kingdom of God as an other-worldly reality, to possess which all were asked to be poor in this world. But Jesus meant something entirely different when he brought the concept of the kingdom of God as the focus and controlling factor of his preaching. Taking a concept from its Old Testament background and its multifaceted understanding in Judaism, Jesus made the kingdom of God the central reality of his preaching, teaching and actions. According to Norman Perrin, the kingdom of God in the ministry of Jesus was a 'tensive symbol', through which Perrin means that it was a concept full of dynamism and vibrations. It was more a symbol than a specific concept which had only its own limited meaning. It means that this concept can take on meanings which can accrue to it from the context, in which it is being realized. The focus of this concept is not on its static subsistence; rather its ability to assume new and contextualized meaning. On the whole, its dynamic meaning is that is a situation of vertical and horizontal relationship in which God is revealed as the *abba*, the Father and Mother, of the entire cosmos, and the entire humankind is presented as a community of the children of God and among themselves they are all sisters and brothers. What this dynamic situation demands is not decided upon a priori; rather it is to be analysed and articulated in each historical, social, economic and cultural context. The kingdom of God is not to be understood spatially and geographically, but operationally as a new situation and as a quality of existence. It is to be understood as a realm of God's continued presence and operation in history. It is a deep symbol which summarizes the entire history of God's presence in the history of Israel, now continued in a much more universal perspective. In fact, Israel's entire history is the framework within which we have to situate the concept of the kingdom of God. Jesus consciously decided to make this symbol of God's kingdom the central theme of his ministry and message. He understood this concept in terms of the definitive coming of God into the history of the whole humankind. The covenant concept with its restricted meaning thus received a universal dimension through the concept of the kingdom of God as embracing the whole humankind and the whole cosmos.

The goal of this new approach of Jesus to God-human relationship was the building up of a new society characterized by equality, harmony and peace. Jesus tried to bring into this new situation all categories of people, many of whom were barred from the traditional Jewish concept of the covenant community. Hence Jesus associated himself with the socially outcast, with the sinners and the tax-collectors. He related himself freely with the Samaritans, with the Gentiles and thereby proved that the kingdom of God is a situation open to all categories of persons. Luke, in particular, takes extra care to show how Jesus was concerned about the poor and the outcast, and he is at the same time very critical of the rich and riches. Writing within the wider context of the Roman Empire, Luke found it necessary to broaden the horizons of God's presence in history beyond the Palestinian context. Living as we are in a world much larger than the Roman empire, we have to understand the whole cosmos and its concerns as belonging to the kingdom of God and the kingdom of God is destined to gradually embrace the entire human history, both political, cultural and religious, and also the whole cosmic and ecological order. It is this one and the same history which Christians are expected to respect and promote as the salvation history embracing the whole humankind and the entire cosmos, in which they have to play a vital role in order to keep it attuned to God's guidance and control. The kingdom of God comes in not to destroy the human kingdom but to transform it and elevate it to new and noble dimensions. It is this history which all Christians are expected to respect and promote as the salvation history, which embraces the whole humankind and the entire cosmos in which they have to play a vital role in order to make it attuned to God's guidance and control. The kingdom of God comes in not to destroy the human kingdom but to transform it and elevate it to new and nobler dimensions.

This approach to the concerns of the kingdom of God and its relation to world history means that all issues in this history are part of the concerns of the kingdom of God, such as the history of all world religions, political history, ideological history, secular movements, ecological movements as well as liberation movements. Any effort to discard some of them as outside the concerns of the kingdom of God is not warranted. All these movements work as God's agents and they all help the Church to have a clearer perception of God who is active in the history of the whole humankind and the whole cosmos. This is to say that world history is the same as salvation history and it is in this broad perspective that we have to understand salvation history and its operation in the world history. The teaching of *Gaudium et Spes* is very relevant: "While we are warned that it profits a man nothing if he gain the whole world and lose himself, the expectation of a new earth must not weaken but rather stimulate our concern for cultivating this one. For here grow the body of a new human family, a body which even now is able to give some kind of foreshadowing of the new age to come. Earthly progress must be carefully distinguished from the growth of Christ's kingdom. Nevertheless, to the extent that the former can contribute to the better ordering of human society, it is of vital concern to the kingdom of God".[12]

Spirit of God active in the World of Matter

The convergence of the sacred and the secular in the understanding of the historical process is given a new and challenging formulation in the theology of Paul when he wrote to the Romans about the final transformation of the material creation through the ongoing activity of the Spirit of the risen Christ (Rom 8:18-25). What we find here is how the entire material creation is included in the plan of God and it is destined to the glory of a final transformation together with the children of God. What is significant about this approach to the secular is the conviction Paul had that the entire material cosmos is destined to participate in the fruits of the resurrection of Christ through which it has been proleptically incorporated into the salvation process. But Paul introduces this idea about the final transformation of the cosmos not from a scientific perspective, but rather from a theological point of view about human suffering and its ultimate meaning in the death and resurrection of Christ. In Rom 8:17 Paul had introduced the idea that the full inheritance of the believers in the Spirit can be had only through a life of intense suffering with Christ. Glory through suffering, life through death, this is the hallmark of Christian life according to Paul. It is the necessary pathway and it is

---

[12] *Gaudium et Spes* art. 39.

unavoidable in view of what the world is. In order to explain the meaning of suffering in view of glory Paul brings in the picture of the general condition of the material creation. The human situation of suffering has something in common with the suffering of the world. In fact, all suffering, all imperfections and all unsatisfied aspirations and longings, of which the traces are so abundant in the external nature as well as within us, do but point forward to a time when all sufferings shall come to an end, all imperfections shall be removed and the frustrated aspirations at last shall be crowned and satisfied.

In this process humans and creation have to encourage each other. The creation encourages humankind insofar as it unfolds itself before them as something into which God has instilled hope, a hope that it will be set free from the bondage to decay and obtain the glorious liberty of the children of God (v. 21). Humans give courage and hope to the creation because in them the creation is privileged to see the beginning of a transformation and glorification, inasmuch as they have the first fruits (*aparche*) of the Spirit, a guarantee of the inheritance that is to come (v. 23). Paul sees in the marks of imperfection on the face of the nature, in the signs at once of high capacities and poor achievement, the visible expression of a sense of something wanting but which will be slowly overcome. It is with this hope of consummation that creation undergoes its subjection to futility and decay. But this consummation will not come by any automatic process of development; it comes through God's own mighty action with universal meaning and cosmic dimensions.

In the midst of this high expectation Paul sees the creation engaged in a chorus of groaning. Before the final glory is revealed the creation suffers like a woman in travail. The image suggests the preparation for a great joy, for the emergence of something altogether new through the crisis of acute and liberating suffering. But faith alone can discern in these phenomena the secret movement which is directing things toward a transcendent goal. If our modern knowledge of the material world yields a very different framework of thought regarding the future of the world, it matters little, provided the essential arguments of Paul are discerned and assimilated. It means that there is an organic relationship between the creation and the human species. Hence the children also join the groaning of the creation inasmuch as they share the destiny of the creation as a whole. A state of patient expectancy is the present condition of the humans who live in the midst of a world of travail, where God also pursues his work with patience. The movement, which draws the humans and all creation towards their intrinsic ends, is gradually realizing the plan of God. No obstacle offered by history will be able to check the work of transformation undertaken by Christ and carried out through his Spirit. Neither the corruptibility of the world and the inward weakness of the humans will prevent God from fulfilling his plans. It is God who is in active control of things. It is not that things will eventually straighten themselves out. God guides them, not with the object of assuring the petty happiness of some people who want to create a paradise for themselves on this planet earth, but with the objective of attaining that salvation and glorification which will be the crown of his work.

Church as the Sacrament of God's Presence in History

Our reflections on God's presence in history enlarging its horizons from the restricted dimensions of the Old Testament to the larger perspectives of human history, which was inaugurated through the ministry and preaching of Jesus, the Emmanuel, come to a critical point where we have to see the Church as founded by Christ having a mission to be the sign and sacrament God's presence in human history taken as a whole. The Dogmatic Constitution on the Church has very clearly formulated this idea when it calls the Church the 'light of the nations' (*Lumen Gentium*). It is not a question of the Church substituting God's presence, but rather it is that the Church derives its vitality and dynamism from God and carries on its mission in the world. Being visible and invisible, earthly and heavenly, this-worldly and other-worldly, the Church must empower herself to carry on this responsible task till the end of history. It is this Church that was rediscovered during the Second Vatican Council, a Church as the servant of the kingdom of God and also the servant of world where she has to be a dynamic presence of the risen Christ, transforming the world through the values of the gospel and the power of the kingdom of God.

Looking back into the history of the Church through the centuries, this mission and task of the Church were not always carried out in fidelity to the mind of Christ and to his gospel. It was not so much God's presence and power that were revealed in her actions and attitudes, but rather her own power and prestige. The Crusades waged by armed pilgrimages and military expeditions, sponsored by the medieval Church from the 11th to the 13th century CE, was a clear proof of the negative attitude of the Church towards other religions. It was a special form of the idea of the just and holy war, which loomed large in the history of the Western piety and thought for many centuries. The Crusades marked a new phase of the barbarian invasions and colonial occupation as well as a spontaneous outburst of pent-up religious ideas. Pope Urban II went to the extent of setting up the Crusades as a definite institution within the history of the Church with indulgences attached to it for those who took part in it. It was associated with the Papal will to power and also it was a special form of missionary zeal to dominate the whole world. Implied in it was also the effort of the Church to work out a Christian ethics of war. Consequently, the Crusades established a turningpoint in religion and spirituality and they always remain as a black mark in the history of the Church.

The 16th century marked the beginning of colonial expansions and occupation of extra-European territory by what are called the 'colonial powers' of Europe, which began with the geographical discoveries of the 16th and 17th centuries and it followed very different courses in respect of politics, economics, religion and sociology. It is all based on the economic, military, and to a great extent cultural superiority of Europe associated with a certain amount of arrogance that was inherited from the Greco-Roman and the early success of Christian civilization, and the colonial powers were fully convinced that they were specially chosen by God to dominate the world. Indigenous cultures were thus underestimated. Colonialism and missionary propaganda went hand in hand. Mission was understood as the expansion of Christianity sponsored and controlled from the West. Christianity assumed an attitude that there was nothing beyond it, that it could control everything, and that it can be the judge of all issues in the world. This phenomenon was to a great extent the result of Christianity understood as identified with the Western powers which continued to control the whole world through their colonial expansion and the accumulation of wealth from the colonized countries, to which were added the large scale missionary expansion work of converting peoples to various Churches with a certain amount of competitive spirit. It is gratifying to see that Pope John Paul II has taken a lead to confess these and similar unholy exercises of the Church in history, for which he apologized to the whole world on March 12, 2000. It is the sincere hope of well-meaning members of the Church that this exemplary step taken by the Pope will characterize the future of the Church in her attitude to the world and to other religions. 'The Church is always in need of a reformation' was a heretical doctrine till recently; but it is now understood as a necessary recognition of the truth about the Church that exists and operates in history. This renewal and inner reformation have to take place through an ongoing *metanoia*, and this is a demanding task and it is part of the costly discipleship and costly grace about which D. Bonhoeffer wrote in his *Cost of Discipleship*.

The ushering in of a new millennium constitutes a new challenge and a salubrious chance for the Church to re-define her role in the world and in history in terms of her important task of being the sign and sacrament of God's presence. The Church at various levels has to analyse and see where she has failed in the past, even as she offers gratitude to God for the great achievements she has made in various areas of her mission in the world. If the Church has to continue her mission as a continuation of the ministry of Christ, she has to re-dedicate herself to the dynamics of service and sacrifice. The Church has to create a new image of her real self and initiate a new thrust to prove that she is faithful to the mission entrusted to her by Christ. She has to assume the role of the little flock that has the assurance from Christ that the Father has been pleased to entrust the kingdom of God to her (Lk 12:32). In order to make this mission effective and meaningful the Church and her members at various levels of their ministry have to become the salt of the earth and the light of the world (Mt 5:13-16). Moreover, the Church has to look and evaluate issues from wider perspectives and relate all things to her transcendent and eschatological goal.

The Dogmatic Constitution on the Church has devoted a chapter to "The Eschatological Nature of the Pilgrim Church and her Union with the Heavenly Church".[13] It refers to the future of the Church and history in terms of the restoration and re-establishment of all things in Christ. The *Pastoral Constitution on the Church in the Modern World* also dwells on the question of history and eschatology in a very realistic perspective. Christ through his life, death and resurrection sums up the meaning of history and he is now at work in the world through the energy of his Spirit, enabling people to look to the future with hope and at the same time animating people to work in the here and now towards that inaugurated future. Hence we understand the importance of human efforts to build a better world and the struggle for justice within the overall eschatological plan of God. This teaching of Vatican II on human development and earthly progress is very important for the way it succeeds in removing the traditional separation of individual and social eschatology, in linking the present with the future and in affirming a unity between the earthly and the heavenly realities. Any interpretation of eschatology that falls short of the requirements of our responsibility toward this world is not a truly Christian understanding of history and eschatology.[14]

God and the Fulfillment of History

Any historical process rooted in time is bound to have its consummation and fulfillment. This is also the biblical approach to history. Deriving inspiration from Trito-Isaiah, the author of the book of Revelation speaks about the end of history through the imagery of a new heaven and a new earth which God would establish at the end of everything, an event that has tremendous significance for the entire historical process which started with the creation of the world. In the language of Trito-Isaiah it was about an apocalyptic event through which the former things would pass away and a new era of prosperity would ensue. It would be like the restoring of the

---

[13] *LG* art. 48-51.

[14] *GS* 39, 43: " The Council exhorts Christians, as citizens of two cities, to strive to discharge their earthly duties conscientiously and in response to the gospel spirit. They are mistaken, who, knowing that we have here no abiding city but seek one which is to come (Hb 13:14), think that they may therefore shirk their earthly responsibilities. For they are forgetting that by the faith itself they are more than ever obliged to measure up to these duties, each according to his proper vocation (2 Thes 3:6-13; Eph 4:28).

original paradise (Gen 2:9; Rev 22: 2,14; Is 11:6-9). The entire scene was centred on the restored Jerusalem (Is 65:9). It would be a restored universe and all would have happiness and there would be no suffering and pain (Is 65: 19b; 25:8). It would be a community of people living in harmony and peace, not only among themselves (Is 65: 21-24) but also with the animal world and the creation at large (Is 65:25).

Confronted by the ongoing persecution by the Roman Empire and threatened by the political situations prevailing in his own times, the author of the book of Revelation also gave articulation to his hope and encouragement to the persecuted Christians of his time through his consoling and assuring words: "Then I saw a new heaven and a new earth, for the first heaven and first earth had vanished, and there was no longer any sea. I saw the holy, new Jerusalem, coming down out of heaven from God, made ready like a bride adorned for her husband. I heard a loud voice proclaim from the throne: 'Now at last God has his dwelling among humans! He will dwell among them and they shall be his people, and God himself will be with them. He will wipe away every tear from their eyes; there shall be an end to death, and to mourning and crying and pain; for the old order has passed away!'. Then he who sat on the throne said, 'Behold! I am making all things new!'" (Rev 21:1-5). The expression 'heaven and the earth' corresponds to the entirety of things and events. Here again it is a scene of prosperity and joy embracing the whole humankind and the whole world.

The most striking aspect of this vision of the eschatological fulfillment of human history as effected through God is the inauguration of a cosmic covenant in which God makes his dwelling place in the human community, taken as a whole: "Now at last God has his dwelling among humans!" It is to be clearly seen that God is not uniting himself with any particular religion, not even with the Church; but rather with the whole of humanity. Religions are only means and at the end of history all religions shall have fulfilled their historical roles. God's ultimate concerns are about the whole humankind irrespective of caste, colour and creed. The expression "They shall be his people and God himself will be with them" is a covenant formula derived from the Old Testament. God established, first of all, a cosmic covenant with Noah promising him that he would never again destroy the earth through a flood and giving him the sign of the "bow in the clouds" which is the sign of universality and wholeness (Gen 9:8-17). Once again, this concluding promise of a cosmic covenant in the book of Revelation at the end of all historical process brings together the whole of humanity, to which God promises his continued presence and on which God sheds his blessings by making it one community of the children of God. It was this universal blessing that God had promised in the beginning when he called Abraham and told him: "In you all the families of the earth shall be blessed" (Gen 12:3). The task and mission entrusted to Abraham was universal.

It is the task and privilege of all living in these critical and blessed times of history to develop a new awareness of God as active in history. At a time when people begin to feel that they are all members of a larger human family and are belonging to a global village, where an unwanted and unwarranted terminology referring to the so-called First, Second and Third Worlds is being gradually avoided because of its bad taste, where religions are trying to transcend their doctrinal and ethical differences in a spirit of appreciation and mutual recognition, it is important that all become responsible to the world and to its historical and ecological process. There is only one history and in it the sacred and the secular, the religious and political, the spiritual and material have their respective roles to play. By creating this cosmos as an intentional expression of his own inner dynamism, God has inaugurated the historical process, a realistic understanding and articulation of which we have in the Bible. This assumption does not mean at all that it is an exclusive understanding of history superior to all other articulations; rather it is a paradigmatic approach and articulation with a message for all. The beauty of this understanding of history will be enhanced through its readiness to accept similar approaches to and articulations of history in the religious books of other living and dynamic religions.

III

HISTORY AND PROPHETIC INVOLVEMENT

The Christian approach to, and understanding of, history are based on the faith conviction that it is controlled and taken care of by God in continuation of the creation of this cosmos and his ongoing and providential care about it through history. In fact, creation itself is the beginning of history. It is from this perspective that we have analysed the world history as a whole basically as salvation history. Since God is one and history is one, so also world history and salvation history are one and the same. God is in complete control of the entire historical process, whether we understand its nature as linear, circular, spiral or cyclic. So also God is the author of history, whether it is political, secular or sacred. At the same time, humans are not just spectators and onlookers of this process. They are called upon to play an active role in this historical process. Though God's plans about history are consistent and convergent, humans taking part in it would sometimes assume roles that are not consistent with God's plans, and hence there can arise conflicts, tensions, confrontations and sometimes wars and the destructive developments in the very process of history. This is precisely what we have been witnessing during the past several hundreds of years. It is here that we see the need of persons who can step in to guide and control the historical process at the religious, social, economic, cultural and political levels. We may call them prophetic persons and the role they play we understand as prophetic involvement. We see a number of them in the Bible, such as Moses and Joshua and the prophets; we see many such prophetic persons in the larger history of humanity and also in the history of the Church. Abraham Lincoln, Martin Luther King, Nelson Mandela and Mahatma Gandhi all belong to this prophetic category. Martin Luther for the Protestant Church and Pope John XXIII for the Roman Catholic Church are powerful examples of prophetic persons who have played significant roles in the shaping of the Church.

Here a word must be said about the very concept of 'prophet' in the biblical sense. Gone are the days when we had understood the prophets as 'foretellers', taking the meaning roughly from the Greek *prophemi*. The Hebrew word *nabi* is most probably derived from the Akkadian *nabu*, which has two interrelated meanings as 'one who is called and also 'one who calls forth'. The former meaning refers to the specific personality of the prophet as one who is personally called by God for a specific task, as against the kings and the priests in the Old Testament who received their office through heredity and right. The second meaning *nabu* refers to what the prophet was supposed to do, namely, to speak forth and proclaim a message in the name of God and thereby to stand on the side of God and defend his cause at all costs. Hence prophets are not primarily foretellers; rather they are forth-tellers, who speak with power and insight. It is such forth-tellers and actors in history who are called prophetic persons and their action in history is associated with prophetic involvement. This is an important dimension for understanding the dynamic nature of history because it is such persons who have changed the course of history and who continue to change the face of history at the religious, social, cultural and political levels. It very often happens that at the time of their prophetic involvement, these prophetic persons are seldom noticed and very often they are rejected as offenders and trouble-makers because they act against conventions and traditions.

When we go through the history of the humankind, we come across several categories of prophetic persons who have played very significant roles in history. One group of these prophetic persons is represented by the prophets of the Old Testament, such as, Jeremiah, Isaiah and Amos. Their mission was to take care of a people committed to God through a covenant, but who had gone away from the ideals of the covenant. Hence Jeremiah was called "to pluck up and to break down, to destroy and to overthrow and then to build and to plant" (Jer 1:10). Their role was critical and creative at the same time. Hence we understand the reluctance of the prophet to respond to his call, saying that he was too young and unskilled to take up the task (Jer 1:6). The second group of prophetic persons is represented by an esoteric group of the Essenes, specifically known as the community of Qumran. Theirs was a prophetic movement of withdrawal and separation from others, very much in revolt against a more secularized form of Judaism during the Hasmonean era, probably during the time of John Hyrcanus, when Judaism became very much independent and was absorbing a lot of secular thinking and living which were not in tune with the Torah religion that was established by Ezra, the father of Judaism. In order to establish an authentic Judaism the Essene community was walking away into the wilderness in protest, claiming that it was the community of the children of light while the rest of the world constituted the children of darkness. They followed a new calendar, adhered to the strict observance of the Torah, led a life of strict discipline till their settlement was destroyed during the Roman attack between 68 and 70 CE.

The third group of prophetic persons is represented by a variety of modern persons, characterized by their social involvement and radical commitment, such as Abraham Lincoln, Mahatma Gandhi and Martin Luther King, Mother Theresa of Calcutta and several other ancient and modern persons. The inner prophetic urge of such persons and the spirit that prompted their social involvement are reflected in a saying attributed to Abraham Lincoln: "I may die any time and I do not know when. But I want it to be said about me by future generations that I have plucked away a weed where I thought I plant would better grow which would eventually produce flowers and fruits and I took care of it and I did plant it". In the long history of the world and in the complex history of the Church we continue to encounter prophetic persons of one or the other kind, namely, those who get involved in history and change the course of history for the good of humanity. Thereby they become immortal and bequeath a message to the future. A Nelson Mandela for South Africa, a Martin Luther for the Church of his times, a Gustavo Gutierrez for the Church in the Latin America, a Pope John XXIII for the Roman Catholic Church, a Mother Theresa of Calcutta for the suffering millions, are all prophetic persons, and the face of history, the face of the Church and the destiny of the society have been radically changed and transformed through the critical and creative role they have played in history. They all issue a call that is addressed to every committed person to become more and more committed to and involved in history and in the events and the issues of history.

Prophets in the History of Israel

In the course of Israel's long and complex history there arose several great and small prophets, whose perception God's word and his involvement in history was deep and profound. This prophetic tradition in Israel had its humble origins during the early years of Israel's history in connection with the deliverance of the people from Egypt. Hence Moses can be properly called a prophet (Hos 12:13). But from the time of Samuel, the word *nabi* was applied to a special class of people in Israel's society. The professional prophets of that day were the immediate forerunners of the great prophets, of whom Elijah came to be regarded as the representative. But the phenomenon began with the emergence of ecstatic prophecy, probably borrowed from the Canaanite environment, and it was known for its often abnormal and frenzied manifestations. These prophets may experience some kind of ecstasy or possession by a spirit at the time of contact with the supernatural power. But very soon prophetism in Israel was transformed into something very sublime and prophets played a very important role in the history of Israel. They were spokespersons of Yahweh in the arena of history.

Among the many characteristics of prophecy in Israel, an important one is that prophetism reflects a Northern Israelite perspective. The major focus of this tradition was a summons to fidelity to the covenant between Yahweh and Israel established at Sinai. The principal figure is Moses as the mediator of this covenant. Scholars believe that this Northern tradition originated during the period of the Judges and was somehow linked with several of the Northern shrines. Its influence is found primarily in the Elohist layer of the Pentateuch, the Deuteronomistic history and the prophetic traditions of Amos, Hosea and Jeremiah. Southern or Judean prophetic tradition, on the other hand, has a distinctly Davidic character and emphasize loyalty to the dynasty and its political and religious institutions. Despite this, all prophetic traditions have come down to us with a marked Deuteronomistic quality to them. These prophetic traditions were probably edited and codified sometime during the exilic or post-exilic period by some prophetic persons with a Deuteronomistic sense of history. Post-exilic prophetic material shows evidence of both Northern and Southern prophetic influence.

The most conspicuous characteristic of prophecy in Israel was its dynamic stance in the affairs of the society, something entirely different from other institutions in Israel, especially kingship and priesthood. Whereas kingship and priesthood were clearly defined institutions that tried to safeguard the political and religions dimensions of the Hebrew society, prophecy in Israel was much more a movement, which was aimed at keeping the holistic dynamism of the nation as a whole. This resulted sometimes in the confrontation between the prophets on the one side and the kings and the priests on the other side. As persons fully aware of their direct and personal call from God, the prophets had their positions clearly defined, and this enabled them always to stand on the side of God, to feel with God, to speak on behalf of God and thereby the guide the nation along the authentic religious traditions transmitted to them from the time of Moses. We may call it an awareness of being called by God or better still as a "God-sensitivity". This aspect of prophetism is very clear in the case of Amos, who had to stand all alone and carry out his mission over against the threat from the priesthood and kingship (Amos 7:10-16). What is significant about this prophetic stance is the firm conviction the prophets had that they were standing for a cause of God, to which they have been committed from the time of their call. Whereas false prophets changed the tone of their prophetic utterance depending on the material advantages they were getting or not getting, the true prophets of Israel had only one cause to stand for, and that was the cause of God. Hence opposition and rejection did not deter them from the execution of their prophetic task.

It is true that some prophets functioned at the heart of the society as significant members of the political or religious establishment. But many others belonged to marginal groups and they addressed the social scene from a less privileged position. Thus both Isaiah and Jeremiah seem to have had access to the king, to whom they gave counsel, while Amos was an outsider, at the shrine of Bethel where he pronounced judgment on Israel and the nations. Their prophetic call might call for a radical social or religious change, or for one that was moderate and gradual. They might press for a return to traditional values and mores or for a steadfast adherence to the *status quo*. Thus Isaiah warned against a foreign allegiance. The language of Isaiah was clear and bold: "Trust in Yahweh; be quiet and keep calm" (Is 7:4). The warning was also clear: "If you do not stand firm in faith (*tha'aminu*), you shall not stand at all(*the'amenu*)" (Is 7:9).Isaiah underscored his message of faith with a characteristic play on Hebrew words and affirmed that the greatest resource in time of trouble is faith, absolute trust in and dependence upon God. Jeremiah encouraged capitulation to Egypt (Jer 38). But he was equally critical of the Temple which he said was no bulwark of security, no guarantee that "God is with us". Jeremiah's sermon created an uproar among the people. Nahum directed his attack against Nineveh, Israel's ancient enemy. The social context out of which and the religious needs to which the prophets spoke, shaped the basic message of the prophets. Hence the word of the prophecy was always a response to a specific social situation in Israel.

Prophets and their Sense of History

By 'sense of history' we mean the power of discernment humans are supposed to have, through which they want to, and are able to understand an event and its implications in the total context of life, to which they are ontologically, ethically and socially related. People who have this sense of history are responsible to all realities connected with the events, especially if these events are having consequences for the life of the people. To live with a sense of history means to be sensitive to human needs, to the problems and concerns of others. People with a sense of history are more socially sensitive and are more interested in the developmental factors of social life. A sense of history brings together people to identical interests, as they foresee future possibilities with some kind of special intuition. For persons having a historical consciousness it is spontaneous to learn from the past and to face the present and the future in the light of the past. For people with a sense of history, history itself is an experience of creativity and an experiment of creating meaning and a mission for themselves. It is a living in the present with a sense of rational sequencing of past, present and future as one continuum. They live in a mode of experiencing the similarity of the three phases of time in one tick of moment. People with a sense of history will not be subjected to the condemnation of repetition of the past. It is those who are not learning from history who are condemned to repeat it. They are people who speak about a third world war because they have not learned from the first and the second world wars. It is against the background of these considerations about the sense of history that we have to look at the prophetic sense of history and its repercussions in the history of Israel. Prophetic involvement in history always presupposes this sense of history, then as well as now.

It seems that the most important characteristic of the prophets of Israel was their sense of history. The prophetic sense of history in Israel could be explained as the capacity of these prophets to see the ongoing movement of the past, present and future as something planned and willed by God. Whereas individuals and groups are always tempted to forget their past in favour of the present, often with a sense of opportunism, and also neglect the future as something beyond their reach, the prophets were committed to the holistic understanding of history as a convergence of the past, present and future, as one inter-related reality. It is true that the present is the only one that is available to humans. The past is gone for ever and the future is beyond one's reach. At the same time, the prophets were more than convinced that it was the past of Israel's history that fashioned their present and that it was that present which would decide and mould the nature of their future. In their efforts to guide the people through the changing vicissitudes of history, the prophets had to make clear to the people that their past was different from that of the others, and consequently, that they were expected to be different from others in their present, and that this awareness of the present alone guaranteed their future. It is precisely in the context of this sense of history that the genuine prophets of Israel were clearly distinguished from the false prophets who were active among the people and who wanted to deceive the kings and the people through wrong guidance given to them in order to have their selfishness and greed fulfilled.

In a certain sense, we have to say that the entire theology of the Old Testament is based on this profound sense of history and at every stage of the formation of the Old Testament we can see this sense of history influencing the various religious and theological traditions of Israel. The remembrance and the recalling of the past was part of the faith tradition of Israel, whether it was their deliverance from Egypt or the making of the covenant on Sinai or their renewed slavery in Babylon. The people were always reminded by the various writers of the Old Testament to be aware of their whole history as something taken care of by God, which had to find its response through their faithful and committed life. The influence of prophetic tradition on the Deuteronomistic tradition is universally accepted among scholars. The people were asked to remember their past and it was the best way to respond to the demands of the present. It is against the background of this appeal to remembrance that we have to understand the inner meaning of the "Little Credo of Israel" (Deut 26:5-10a),[1] a confession made by the members of the people of Israel on the occasion of the offering of the first fruits of their land, when they were living in the land of Canaan. The spirit of this Credo is basically that of grateful believer who recognizes everything as God's gifts. Here the Israelites recall the entire history of Israel from the time of Jacob onwards, who is presented as a wandering Aramean. The speaker rehearses the chain of the acts of salvation by God from Jacob onwards up to the entry into Canaan. It confines itself to recalling the

---

[1] It was G. von Rad who first suggested this designation for this passage, meaning thereby that it somehow corresponds to the Christian Credo, in which the salvation events related to Christian faith are summarized and confessed.

most essential and basic facts. In Deut 26:9 the recital of the historical facts comes to an end. With v. 10 the speech becomes very personal, for the speaker now puts himself into the situation of which he has recounted the historical background. It is important to realize that the fruits he has to offer come from the ground which the Lord has given him. Thereby it brings out the dynamic meaning and message of remembrance Moses asked Israel to maintain and cherish.

The most significant nature of this recital is the profound awareness the Israelites had about their low and humble beginnings and the readiness on their part to attribute all what they were and all what they had to their own God who empowered them and made them prosper. They acknowledged that they were only a marginalized group of people who had nothing to claim for themselves. They did not forget their roots even as they harvested their fruits. They confessed: "The Lord heard our voice and saw our affliction, our toil and our oppression". Now that they enjoy the blessings of the land flowing with milk and honey, it was only natural that they brought the first fruits of the land to their God as a mark of their gratitude to God and also to experience for themselves how much they depended on their God for what they were and what they had. It was a joy for them to recall and recount the blessings of God they had received throughout their history. It is another story whether they kept up this spirit of gratitude towards God. But the basic point is that the biblical writers have taken pain to establish the foundational realities of their religion through such a bold and noble confession related to their history.

In fact, Moses is presented in the book of Deuteronomy as exhorting the people before they entered the Promised Land that they should always remember what God had done for them. He reminded them: "When you have eaten your fill and have built fine houses and live in them, when your herds and flocks have multiplied, and your silver and gold is multiplied, and all that you have is multiplied, then do not exalt yourself, forgetting the Lord your God, who brought you out of the land of Egypt, out of the house of slavery, who led you through the great and terrible wilderness, an arid wasteland with poisonous snakes and scorpions. He made water flow for you from flint rock, and fed you in the wilderness with manna that your ancestors did not know, to humble you and to test you, and in the end to do you good. Do not say to yourself, 'My power and the might of my own hand have gotten me this wealth'. But remember the Lord your God, for it is he who gives you power to get wealth, so that he may confirm his covenant that he swore to your ancestors, as he is doing today" (Deut 8:12-17). For Israel, remembrance was not a mere psychological recalling of past events; rather it was a dynamic exercise of their faith and trust in God, through which they had to get ready for the challenge of the present and the future.

The application of this sense of history in Israel is so profound that, recalling the great event of the making of the covenant on Sinai, Moses could speak to the people gathered in the plains of Moab that God entered into that covenant not with their ancestors, but with them who were expected to live up to the demands of that covenant. Since their ancestors who had entered into covenant were now dead, it was the duty of those who were alive to respond to the spirit and the demands of that covenant: "The Lord our God made a covenant with us at Horeb. Not with our ancestors did the Lord make this covenant, but with us who are all of us here alive today. The Lord spoke with you face to face at the mountain, out of the fire" (Deut 5:2-4). Through this re-living of history Moses made the people of Israel realize the impact their history has on their life and activities who were preparing themselves to enter the Promised Land. Since they had inherited their present from their past, it was necessary for them to remember and re-relive the demands of the past in a manner that would make them realize the profound significance of that past for the whole process of their present and future history.

The prescriptions in the books of Leviticus and Deuteronomy about Sabbath, Sabbath Year and the Jubilee Year are also to be understood as related to this sense of history. Before we can specify some salient perspectives of this great event, it is important that we see the background of these traditions. The origin and spirit of the Jubilee Year was related to the prescription about the observance of the Sabbath in Israel, a day that was to be set apart by all Israelites, their slaves and their animals, to rest and to keep away from all kinds of work (Ex 23:12; 34:12). The creation narrative of the Yahwist in Genesis 2:2 refers to Sabbath as a day of God's rest after his creative action, through which he completed his work, and this cosmic event is the theological basis for Israel's rest. This divinely initiated rest should teach the Israelites how after they had worked for six days, they should transcend their work and belong to the realm of God's rest (Ex 20:8-10). The accent of this rest was not so much on the physical rest; but rather on the inner message of training the people to see their work not as their ultimate mission in this world. They had to work in order to participate in the creative work of God; but they had also to transcend this world through their rest. To this prescription work and rest there were added also humanitarian motifs in course of time. Later on, the nature of the Sabbath rest was the subject of much casuistic discussion by the rabbis, and on this point Jesus had very often to come into conflict with much of their interpretation In that context Jesus had to say: "The Sabbath is made for humans and not humans for the Sabbath" (Mk 2:27), thereby pointing to the inner meaning and message of this religious practice.

Based on this biblical tradition of sabbatical rest, we see also the evolution of a sabbatical year in three books of the Old Testament: Ex 23:10-11; Deut 15:1-3 and Lev 25:2-8. The cycle of seven years is obviously inspired by the week of seven days, ending in the sabbatical rest. The book of Exodus and Leviticus agree on the substance of the sabbatical prescriptions; the law requires that the land should not be cultivated, but is to lie fallow during the seventh year. Like humans and animals, it also is to have a Sabbath rest. God pledged his extra blessings during the sixth year, the produce of which will enable them to live through the year of the fallow and the next year too, till the forthcoming harvest (Lev 25:18-22). Moreover, during that year the natural produce of the fields was to be left for the poor (Ex 23:10-11). The law in Deuteronomy 15:1-3,9 is not directed to the land and does not speak of a Sabbath or rest; it is a law directing that debts should be remitted after seven years. The directive of Deuteronomy 15:9 implies that a regular cycle of seven years is meant. Alienation of family property and the development of lending at interest led to the growth of pauperism and the enslavement of defaulting debtors or their dependents. This destroyed that social equality which had existed at the time of the tribal federation and which still remained as an ideal. The remission of debts should occur every seventh year, and then all persons who have been enslaved for non-payment of a debt were set free (Deut 15:1-6). The slaves were insolvent debtors who have soled themselves or have been sold, and setting them free involved writing off the debt. It also prescribed that no one may refuse a loan to his poorer brothers and sisters, thinking: 'Soon it will be seventh years, the year of remission' (Deut 15:9). It is not altogether certain whether the sabbatical year is connected with another law found in Ex 21:2-6 and Deut 15:12-14 which prescribed that a Hebrew slave was to be given his choice of freedom or continued enslavement in the seventh year of his servitude.

The grand sabbatical year, known as the Jubilee Year, was celebrated every fiftieth year, and it was a multiplication of seven sabbatical years, the details of which are given in Leviticus 25:8-55. The name 'Jubilee' is derived from the Hebrew *yobel*, meaning a ram's horn, which was used as a trumpet to announce the inauguration of the Jubilee year (Lev 25:9). The year was to begin on the Day of Atonement and was a period of emancipation in which, in addition to the usual sabbatical observance (Lev 25:11-12), all alienated property was to be returned to its original owner (Lev 25:10,13). The basic principle guiding the whole discussion about the details of the Jubilee Year in Israel is this: The land belongs to God and it is entrusted to the Israelites as a result of the covenant. The Psalmist solemnly professes: "The earth is the Lord's and all that is in it; the world and those who live in it" (Ps 24:1). So also the underlying idea is that the impoverished, who had to risk their future for the sake of survival, are also belonging to God and they cannot be ill-treated for ever. They must be periodically rehabilitated so that they can also live in dignity as the people of God. On the whole, the picture given here of the socio-economic organization of Israel was something unique and grandiose.

It is the considered view of biblical scholars that these laws about social justice represent a meaningful and excellent ideal rather than a law that was put into practice during the history of Israel. No reference in the Old Testament suggests that these details were ever put into practice as such. Although we cannot exclude the possibility of its being observed during the early years of the land's occupation by the Twelve Tribal Confederacy before it came under the monarchy, its presence in these books of the Old Testament is best explained as a social blueprint, founded on the deeply religious concepts of justice and equality, as formulated in the covenant law. It was drawn up and added to the books of Exodus, Deuteronomy and Leviticus probably during the period after the exile. Although the details of these laws were not realized according to the letter of these prescriptions, its spirit of appreciation for personal rights and human dignity synthesizes much of Old Testament teaching and it has a great message for our times. It would seem that these so-called primitive people without much of modern education as well as informative technology could envisage an egalitarian society much better than what is being achieved in our times where many nations have to be impoverished for a few nations to live in luxury. On the top of these, the evils of globalization and market economy are only adding to the misery of these nations. What we need is a sense of history similar to the one the people of Israel had. On account of some unfortunate historical reasons and paradoxes, such as the colonialism engineered from the West, humanity has been divided into a permanent division of haves and have-nots and nothing worthwhile has been done so far to remove and eradicate this perpetual scandal of history. National and International consultations take place from time to time to discuss issues related to sustainable development. But they never venture to touch the core of the problems. Politics will never take any step to solve any of these problems and religions are afraid to venture on it.

Prophets and the Secular Dimension of Religion

The above reflections on the secular dimensions of the covenant community of Israel invite us to analyse the concerns of the prophets of the Old Testament to make the community of Israel respond to the demands of the covenant in their socio-economic life. In fact, what James wrote centuries later about true religion has its basis in the teaching of many of the pre-exilic prophets. James wrote: "Religion that is pure and undefiled before God, the Father, is this: to care for orphans and widows in their distress, and to keep oneself unstained by the world" (James 1:27). It is precisely this that Isaiah emphasized in the context of his criticism of the externalism of cult in the

Southern Kingdom: "Wash yourselves clean; remove the evil of your doings from before my eyes; cease to do evil, learn to do good, seek justice, rescue the oppressed, defend the orphan, plead for the widow" (Is 1:16-17). Starting with Elijah, it was the task of the prophets to guide the course of Israel's history, very often against the collective will of the established hierarchy of kingship and priesthood. It is significant that we read in the book of kings about Elijah undertaking a journey to Sinai, where Moses had received the revelation from Yahweh about the life and activities of the covenant community. In a certain sense, the whole prophetic movement, of which Elijah is a pioneer, was a pilgrimage back to Sinai, to the sources of Israel's original faith. The prophets did not claim to be innovators, who came forth with some bright new ideas that would enable Israel to keep their history up-to-date in the onward march of culture. Rather, they demanded that Israel return to the wholehearted covenant allegiance demanded by Yahweh. They were reformers who took their stand on the ancient ground of Sinai. But in a deeper sense the prophetic movement was not a kind of archaism, a timid response to cultural crisis. In the message of the prophets the Mosaic past came alive in the present with new vitality and meaning. What was latent in the Mosaic tradition began to come to fullness, and Israel was given a deeper understanding of the implications of the covenant and Yahweh's ways in history. Thus the Naboth incident (1 Kgs 21:1-16), in which Ahab and his Phoenician wife Jezebel were involved, provides an excellent preface to the social message of the prophets of a later period.

The great Israelite prophets were champions of the stern ethical demands of the ancient Mosaic tradition. Israel's covenant obedience was motivated by gratitude for the great acts of redemption that Yahweh had wrought on behalf of his oppressed people. Yahweh had created a covenant community in which all stood equal before the law, whether they were rich or poor, kings or private citizens. The whole community was responsible to the sovereign will of Yahweh as expressed in the laws that had been handed down from the wilderness period and refined by legal usage. When the justice of few was downtrodden by the powerful, Yahweh intervened to defend the weak and the defenseless and to restore the order and solidarity of the covenant community. Baalism tended to support the *status quo*, with the aristocracy on top. But the Yahweh faith, as revived by the prophets, supplied the energy for a protest against the evils of commercial civilization for social reformation. Thus, when the northern kingdom reached the zenith of material prosperity during the reign of Jeroboam II, economic injustice thrived. As a result, Samaria, its luxurious capital, became the centre of wealth and an oppressive social pyramid grew up with the royal courtiers and the merchant class at the top and the great mass of people ground into poverty at the bottom. The heinous crime committed by Ahab against Naboth was perpetrated on a wider scale, as economic tyrants with the sanction of corrupt courts (Am 5:10-13) "sold the righteous for silver, and the needy for a pair of shoes" (Am 2:6; cf. 8:4-6). Amos felt that these crimes would have been shocking to any of Israel's neighbours with an elementary sense of justice (cf. Am 3:9-10). The prophetic books of Amos and Hosea give a clear picture of the social injustice practised in Israel. Amos pointed out the social injustices of his day with such severity that Amaziah regarded his message as high treason. Wealthy merchants, lusting for economic power, were ruthlessly trampling on the heads of the poor and the defenseless. Public leaders, reveling in luxury and corrupted by indulgence, were lying in beds of ease. The sophisticated ladies were selfishly urging their husbands on an easy life. Law courts were used to serve the vested interests of the commercial class. Religion had no word of protest against the inhumanities that were being perpetrated in the very shadow of the temples of Bethel, Gilgal, Dan and Samaria. To Amos, all these things were symptoms of a deep 'sickness unto death'. It is in similar circumstances during the time of Manasseh that we hear another prophet, Micah, voicing his concerns about a covenanted people: "What does Yahweh require of you but to do justice, and to love kindness, and to walk humbly with your God?" (Mic 6:8).

It is in the midst of these developments that the prophets, as the checkpots of Israel's history, voiced their concern for the future of Israel in terms of threats and promises, but always standing on the side of God, ultimately articulating their optimism of grace. While Proto-Isaiah sees this bright future in terms of a restored Davidic dynasty (Is 7:14; 9:2-6; 11:1-9), Deutero-Isaiah sees the Servant of the Lord (Is 42:1-7; 49:1-7; 50:4-9; 52:13-53:12) purifying the nation through his elevated personality and Trito-Isaiah speaks of the one who is anointed by God to bring good news to the poor and the oppressed, to bind up the brokenhearted and to proclaim liberty to the captives and release to the prisoners (Is 61:1-3). Jeremiah announced the inauguration of a "new covenant" of inner renewal and interiority (Jer 31:31-34) and Ezekiel described the new era of the spirit and the heart (Ezek 11:17-20; 36:26-28). The most important aspect of the mission these prophetic persons is that they wanted to see history as fully taken care of by God even if human malice and lack of faith and justice on the part of Israel seemed to thwart God's plans. In fact, there was no question of a history left to its own destiny. It is this prophetic sense of history that was to be carried on into the history of the early Church with new overtones and new challenges.

Prophetic leaders in the Early Church

Our discussion about the prophetic tradition in the Old Testament as something committed to its sense of history which is spread out in the various books of the Old Testament would remain incomplete if we do not analyse some books of the New Testament, especially the Acts of the Apostles, which also present the prophetic role played by some authentic leaders in the early Church with their powerful sense of history. Though the Acts of the Apostles apparently is interested in presenting the early Church as a very inspiring and ideal community committed to the gospel, first of all preached by Jesus of Nazareth, a close analysis of this book shows that it was not the case at all. The early Church was a Church in crisis because it had to discover it is own identity in the context of ideological conflicts. The problem was not about the message that was committed to the Church and her leaders by Jesus, rather it was a question of how they understood it and wanted to put it into practice. Though Jesus envisaged only one kind of mission that would embrace the whole world within the larger context of his announcement of the kingdom of God, the leaders in the early Church were somehow forced to conceive of two missions: one run from Jerusalem, with Peter and the Sons of Zebedee in charge, and later James, Jesus' brother, and other members of his family; and the other run by Paul, first of all from Antioch and later on from various centers in Asia Minor and Greece. The two missions were agreed about the supreme significance of Jesus, but they disagreed about almost everything else. It is true that the New Testament, as a whole, gives the impression of a united, developing body of belief and practices because it is a selection of writings. Naturally, it was selected by the winning mission, that is the Paulines, and that is why it consists of many letters of Paul and four Gospels, two of which are very much Pauline, namely, Luke and John, and the other two building bridges to Jerusalem.

It is within the framework of this critical history of the early Church that we have to see the role played by prophetic leaders who were determined to hold on to the original message of Jesus of Nazareth and were ready to take up a critical stance against the pro-Jewish understanding of the message of Jesus. Over against the idyllic picture of the Jerusalem Church as a community characterized by inner and external harmony (Acts 2:42-47; 4:32-35), we see tensions and crises growing up among the Jewish Christian members because of cultural differences among them, and this is described in the story of the widows in Jerusalem (Acts 6:1-6). As one elected by the community to serve it with prudence and fairness, Stephen, one of the seven, realized that the ultimate problem in this crisis was deeper than cultural differences. It was more a question of a sectarian understanding of the religious movement inaugurated by Jesus of Nazareth, and Stephen wanted to safeguard the truth and integrity of the gospel against all sectarian thinking. Hence he had to become a controversial figure in the early Church, apparently calling his own identity into question. As the first authentic witness (*martys*) to Christ, it was also his fate to undergo these oppositions which Jesus himself had to face from his opponents and adversaries. Beyond that, Stephen's witnessing to Christ involved the same critical attitude of Jesus towards the Jewish Torah and the Jerusalem Temple. It is paradoxical to see that Stephen was criticizing the very same Temple which Peter and John as well as the other disciples of Jesus were visiting several times during the day for their official prayers (Acts 3:1; 2:46). For the first time there was an inner polarization between the Christian community and Judaism. For the first time the Church had to define her inner nature and establish her identity independent of Judaism. Stephen had the courage to do that, but at the cost of his own life. His bearing witness to Christ meant for him the need to stand for all the values which Jesus had already introduced through his earthly ministry and to establish which he had to undergo the reality and scandal of the death on the cross. Stephen also had to face this fate in his being stoned to death (Acts 7:59-60). As the author of the letter to the Hebrews writes, Jesus had to die outside the camp in order to sanctify the people and hence he exhorted his readers also go outside the camp in order to bear witness to him (Heb 13:12-13). Stephen, the first witness of Jesus, had the courage to go outside the myopic camp of a sectarian Christianity at Jerusalem, which was controlled by the Twelve, in order to bear witness to Christ and thus to liberate the Church of the future from all kinds of sectarian thinking.

The Stephen episode initiated a new wave of tension and conflict between the Hellenistic Christians and the Jews which is narrated in the Acts of the Apostles. It seems that Paul was mainly responsible for the killing of Stephen because it is narrated that the witnesses against Stephen laid their coats at his feet (Acts 7:58) and that he approved of the stoning of Stephen (Acts 8:1a), which indications are powerful enough in the context of what Luke has to say later on about the reverse role Paul played in the future history of the Church. In the beginning Paul persecuted the Christian movement, which was supposedly a sectarian group confessing a crucified Jesus as the Messiah, much against the basic belief in Judaism. But Stephen had gone a step further when he emphasized that Judaism had only a relative role to play in history and that the Christ event was something transcending and fulfilling the history of Israel, a doctrine Paul was not at all ready to accept until he encountered the risen Jesus on his way to Damascus. The prophetic role played by Stephen in the early Church resulted in a severe persecution of the Christians by the Jews. Were all Christians persecuted? It would appear that only the Hellenistic Christians were the main target of the persecution. In fact, in Acts 8:1b it is clearly stated that the apostles in Jerusalem were not persecuted. If all Christians were persecuted, why were the apostles spared? The reasons seems to be the following: Firstly, the author of the Acts found it necessary to see the Jerusalem Church continuing to exist and operate through the presence of the apostles, and secondly, because the apostles themselves were not a problem for the official Judaism, except that they had the courage to confess the risen Christ as the Messiah. In fact, the apostles were a more a pro-Jewish group, and probably they were not very happy with the stance taken by Stephen towards Judaism. From the human point of view, Stephen acted imprudently. For many, Stephen was a person who was a trouble-maker and so he was to be eliminated.

But the crisis that resulted from this persecution was a beneficial one for the future of the Christian movement. It was a time for the wider diffusion of the power of the Spirit, which had got powerfully started through Stephen. The Hellenistic group, characterized by its centrifugal power, began to take advantage of this situation. Although not authorized by the official Church of Jerusalem, Philip, one of the seven servants of the table, went and preached the gospel among the Samaritans, the bitter enemies of the Jews. But the mission of Philip was a big success, as it is reported in the Acts: "The crowd paid great attention to the words of Philip as he spoke to them and saw the wonders he had performed" (Acts 8:6). In fact, this mission among the Samaritans was part of the programme of witnessing the risen Jesus had entrusted to his disciples (Acts 1:8). The real outcome of this commission should have been that the apostles would never have taken the initiative for this delicate risk, because of their psychological aversion toward the Samaritans. But God's plans about the future of the gospel should not in any way be controlled by human resistance and so also the ways of accomplishing them. What is noteworthy here is the encouraging and positive reaction of the official Church in Jerusalem towards what Philip had accomplished. Not only that the Jerusalem Church did not place any *moratorium* on the work of Philip, but rather it sent Peter and John to approve of the work of Philip (Acts 8:14-17). They went and prayed over the converted Samaritans. Philip was only a layperson; but it is was this layperson who was responsible for taking the gospel outside of the Jewish territory and make it available to the Samaritans. It seems that the daring act of Philip to preach the gospel to the Samaritans prompted Peter and John also to go back to Jerusalem, on the way preaching to the same Samaritans: "They returned to Jerusalem, proclaiming the good news to many villages of the Samaritans" (Acts 8:25). Although the persecution of the Christians in Jerusalem constituted an apparent setback for the progress of the gospel, as a matter of fact, in a more mysterious manner, it promoted the spread of the gospel into the wider world.

The role played by Philip in preaching the gospel is further enhanced by the fact that it is also he who was inspired by the Spirit of God to admit the Ethiopian official into the community of the believers (Acts 8:26-39). Through this daring action Philip, the lay missionary, once again inaugurated the far more challenging mission of the Church among the Gentiles. In fact, in course of time this would become a crucial issue for the Church to approach. But in the case of Philip this admission of the Gentile is described as a simple event. This invitation given to him to admit the Ethiopian official into the community of the believers gave Philip a new impetus to preach the gospel in the north-western part of Palestine, such Azotus and Caeasarea where Gentiles lived in large numbers (Acts 8:40). We do not know whether the Jerusalem Church ever came to know about it. But Luke has shown his wisdom and theological insight to draw a broad framework for the missionary work of the early Church through the initiative of a lay leader, who was also an unauthorized missionary. As a theologian of history Luke has taken great care to establish that the history of the early Church was more in the hands of God than in the myopic vision of the authorities of the Jerusalem Church.

The Gospel for the Wider World

The story of the conversion of Cornelius is the longest single event narrated in the Acts with 66 verses (Acts 10:1-11:18) with many repetitions and it is so because of the decisive significance of this event for the entire theology of the Acts and for the future of the Church. The full significance of this story is that the author wants to establish a clear doctrine about God's definitive and ultimate decision about accepting the Gentiles into the Church in spite of the fact that Peter, the leader of the Twelve, was resisting it right through. The paradox of this story is that in the case of the Ethiopian official Philip, a layperson, was not only willing to act as directed by the angel of the Lord, whereas in the case of Cornelius, Peter, the leader of the chosen disciples of Jesus, who were supposed to have understood the mind of Jesus better, was resisting the divine initiative to the last point till God persuaded him to his side. Hence the main characteristic of this story is the divine compulsion overcoming the human resistance. Peter is fully convinced of his being clean and holy, while for him others are unclean and unholy (Acts 10:14; 11:8). But God sees everything and everyone from a different perspective. Hence God declares: "What God has declared clean, you should not call unclean" (Acts 10:15; 11:9). It ultimately means that God has taken up the entire responsibility of what was going to happen. Peter had to first undergo a radical conversion in his whole evaluative system before he could convert Cornelius and enable him to fulfill his religious aspirations. The result of this divine intervention is that not only Cornelius is converted, but the whole family of Cornelius (Acts 10:44-48). This is followed by the story of the outpouring of the Holy Spirit, the Pentecost of the Gentiles. Once and for all, Peter was convinced that God's gifts are not the exclusive privilege of a certain section of people and that God can extend his saving grace to all those whom he wants. Hence Peter became strong in his conviction and he was bold enough to convince his adversaries in Jerusalem when they questioned him about the propriety of his action. His words were strong and uncompromising: "If God gave them the same gift that he gave us when we believed in the Lord Jesus Christ, who was I that I could hinder God?"(Acts 11:17). It was a prophetic voice and its repercussions are now being heard throughout the world, especially in countries like India where the Church continues to exercise her ministry in the midst of religious pluralism.

What happened in the Jerusalem Church was only a preparation for more radical developments in the future of the Church in new community of the disciples of Christ in Antioch, a Church that was founded by Hellenistic Christians who were scattered in connection with the persecution after the killing of Stephen (Acts 11:19-26). It seems that this Church had among its members both Jewish and Gentile Christians. The reference to a "great number of believers who *turned* (*epestrpsen*) to the Lord" (Acts 11:21) would mean that it is about the conversion of the Gentiles. It means that the entire makeup of the Church of Antioch was different from that of the Jerusalem Church. Consequently, it was with a sense of surprise that the leaders of the Jerusalem Church heard about the foundation of this new Church in a new area without the knowledge of the Jerusalem Church. But they did the wise thing, as in the case of the Samaritan mission undertaken by Philip, by sending Barnabas, who was also a Hellenistic Christian and who could better understand the situation in the Hellenistic environment of Antioch. With his better insight into the nature and future of this community, Barnabas brought Saul also to Antioch, and Paul was at this time passing through a state of oblivion back at home because of the suspicion he had to face from the Jews as well as from the Christians in Jerusalem. Barnabas and Paul together built up a dynamic Church at Antioch which had to play a significant and decisive role in the future history of early Church. This Church had a very cordial relationship with the mother Church at Jerusalem and as a sign of it the Jerusalem Church was helped by the Church of Antioch during a time of economic need (Acts 11:28-30). At the same time, in a more important issue of sending Barnabas and Paul for their mission of preaching the gospel among the Gentiles, the Church of Antioch did not even consult the Jerusalem Church, much less obtain its prior permission, and it was felt that this was not necessary at all, because the Holy Spirit had taken the initiative for such a bold action. Acts 13:1-3 state that the Holy Spirit had directed the prophetic leaders in the community to send two of its best persons, Barnabas and Saul, for a mission of preaching the gospel among the Gentiles. In fact, this Church had a greater readiness and openness to reach out to the Gentiles. Hence the community fasted and prayed, laid their hands on Barnabas and Saul, and sent them off. As a mark of the real change that took place in the life of Saul through this mission, the author of the Acts from now onward fixed on Saul his Greek name 'Paul' (Acts 13:9), in fulfillment of his role as the apostle of the Gentiles.

The first missionary journey of Paul and Barnabas was a great success, as we read in Acts 13:14- 14:28. It has also be observed that the accent on the mission among the Gentiles became clear to them only after they realized that the Jews in the Diaspora also rejected the gospel. At the conclusion of the speech to the Jews in Antioch of Pisidia on a Sabbath Paul and Barnabas realized that their mission among the Jews was still a problematic one because the Jews were still objecting to the gospel they preached. Hence they had to take a new decision: "It was necessary that the word of God should be spoken first to you. Since you reject it and judge yourselves to be unworthy of eternal life, we are now turning to the Gentiles" (Acts 13:46). By contrast, when the Gentiles heard this, they were glad and they praised the word of the Lord (Acts 13:48). Thereby the Church became a universal reality. The centrifugal force released by Stephen and Philip kept on growing, until through Paul the gospel became a fully liberated and liberating power ready to embrace the whole humankind. The crisis of growth inaugurated by Stephen and further carried on by Philip proved itself to be the right course of action to happen in order to make the gospel, once inaugurated by Jesus of Nazareth, become a transforming power for the whole world. In fact, the Spirit of the risen Lord guided this process; at the same time, it was to be assisted by some individuals who had the wisdom and the courage to discern God's plans and guide it to a great success.

Paul's Prophetic Stance in the Early Church

Luke, the theologian of history, after guiding his readers through a series of historical happenings which ultimately realized God's plans, at one stage stops to narrate an event which should be seen as the most serious crisis in the early Church. But the timely and prophetic involvement of Peter and Paul averted the crisis for some time. The story has two versions, one by the author of the Acts (Acts 15:1-12) and the other by Paul in his letter to the Galatians (Gal 2:1-10). Paul and Barnabas had returned to Antioch after their first successful mission among the Gentiles and a new atmosphere of freedom and peace was evident all over the area when the gospel regained its transcendent power as available to all. All on a sudden, a major and unexpected attack came from some members in the Jerusalem Church who questioned the validity of the mission undertaken by the Church in Antioch through the initiative of the Holy Spirit. Some believers from Jerusalem went down to Antioch and began to argue that Gentile Christians were also to be circumcised and directed to observe the prescriptions of the Mosaic law just like the Jewish Christians. The implied idea in this approach was that these persons wanted to keep the Christian movement as a sect within Judaism. For them it was more a question of accommodating one more sect within the larger reality of Judaism which was made up of a number of sects and groups, sometimes one opposed to the other.

As it happened in the case of the problem of the widows (Acts 6:1-6), here again an official and practical solution to the problem had to be reached. It was the basic question about the identity of the Christian movement in relation to Judaism. Externally seen, it was all about the question of admitting the Gentiles into the Church without circumcision and the observance of the Torah.

While Paul and Barnabas had preached a gospel according to which the Gentile Christians were not bound by these Jewish practices, some influential Jewish Christians insisted on the need of obeying these Jewish prescriptions. The author of the Acts had already prepared his readers for a healthy solution to the problem through his long story of Cornelius where there was no question of any circumcision. It was all question of baptism and the outpouring of the Holy Spirit in the entire family of Cornelius. Hence here again Peter intervenes by stating that no further restrictions should be placed on the Gentile Christians. Apparently the problem was once and for all solved in the Jerusalem Council (Acts 15:1-12). What we read in the second part of Acts 15; 13-29 seems to be a event which happened many years later, when James, the brother of the Lord, had assumed office as the head of the Jerusalem Church and Peter had left Jerusalem or were forced to leave Jerusalem because of the increasing influence of James and his pro-Jewish approach to the Christian movement. This meeting was presided over by James in which several restrictions were placed on Gentile Christians for facilitating table fellowship between Jewish and Gentile Christians. The Gentile Christians were happy to abide by these restrictions because thereby they could experience a little more of equality with the Jewish Christians, though practically they were treated as second class Christians. It was a sad phenomenon very much opposed to the policy of Paul (Gal 3:28; Col 3:10-11) and this attitude continued to exist in the history of the Church in various forms for many more centuries.

What Luke has explained as the Jerusalem Council with Peter as the spokesperson and the final authority, has received another version in the writings of Paul and it is the opinion of many scholars that in Gal 2:1-10 Paul is referring to the same event in his own words. Here the accent of the story is on the decisive role played by Paul in the Jerusalem council, much against the general trend in Jerusalem. Paul had to fight single-handed to safeguard the truth about the gospel and he did not give in to any human interference because he was a convinced and committed person. Because of Paul's strong stance, there emerged a compromise formula about the future mission of the Church, according to which Peter and others would go for a Jewish mission while Paul and Barnabas would concentrate on a mission among the Gentiles. Although the details of this narrative are very much different from that of the Acts of the Apostles, the main conclusion of the story about the freedom of the Gentile Christians stands out clearly in both narratives. Considering the inner nature of this issue from a psychological and cultural point of view, it would appear that the credit of this decision goes more to Paul than to Peter.

The crisis that started in the early Church with the problem of the widows in Jerusalem (Acts 6:1-6) kept on taking new forms until a final crisis threatened to destroy the whole work of Jesus of Nazareth. Thanks to the prophetic involvement of some gifted leaders, every time a solution was reached. But the issue of the diversified qualities of the Jewish and Gentile Christianity always remained a burning issue during the following years also. It is a tragedy of history that people never learn from the past. Religious fundamentalism has its own ways of repeating the past under the pretext of respecting tradition. Some tend to repeat the mistakes which once proved to be dangerous. But Paul had realized for himself that the past he had given up in favour of a better present and future should never be repeated. As a man of conviction and commitment, he always remained faithful to the prophetic call he had received from God. It meant sufferings and rejection for Paul. But he was not discouraged. He had his faith and trust in God and in the power of the risen Christ. Moreover, the bold stance taken by Paul in his liberal attitude toward the Gentile Christians resulted in the leaders in the Church of Jerusalem developing a negative attitude towards the very person of Paul and also towards the collection he had organized for the poor Christians in Judea among the Churches of the Gentile Christians at the request of these leaders of the Jerusalem Church (Gal 2:10). Hence Paul wrote to the Christians in Rome to pray for him so that the offerings he had collected from those Churches with much difficulty (1 Cor 16:1-4; 2 Cor 8:1-9:15) may be acceptable to the leaders in the Church of Jerusalem (Rom 15:31).

Prophetic Persons in the Church: Their Role in our Times

The above analysis of history and prophetic involvement in the history of Israel and in the history of the early Church shows that the biblical religion had to go through a series of crises before it could become a meaningful religious movement which could guide its members in their mission in the world. The Church in our times also passes through a series of crises and this is true of all Churches. What is important is that we should have a positive approach in the face of these crises because they belong to the very dynamics of growth. It is the all the more so because the Church is not a mere human institution. It is at the same time divine and human, visible and invisible, this-worldly and other-worldly, and it could very often happen that the human, the visible and the this-worldly obscure the divine, the invisible and the other-worldly, and sometimes they try to blur and extinguish the divine and the invisible. It is painful to face these crises, but it is inevitable. Paul was referring to the crises in the Church of Corinth in the celebration of the Lord's Supper and he concluded his observation with an optimistic note: "It is good that there are factions among you" (1 Cor 11:18) because factions and crises reveal who are genuine and who are not genuine. What we very much need today is the presence of women and men, characterized by wisdom and having a share in the Spirit of God, who not only initiate crises but also guide them to a successful outcome in such a way that the Church can emerge as the real servant of the kingdom of God. The prophets of the Old Testament, Stephen, Philip and Paul were all characterized by this wisdom as well as a dynamic sharing in the Spirit of God, and they invite us to do the same in our times, not for the sake of crises themselves but for the good results that have to result from these crises.

The history of the Church during these past several centuries also has witnessed several prophetic persons who have changed the face of the Church and the course of history through their prophetic involvement. But it is true that precisely at the time of their involvement some of these persons were suspected as heretics and destroying the inner reality of the Church. But time has proved that they were right. Having been committed to truthfulness, these prophetic persons found the need of articulating their convictions on sensitive issues related to theology and praxis. Now also there are many theologians who are aware of the results of historical and other critical studies, but at certain crucial points they try to accommodate and arrive at a compromise for their application to Christian doctrine. In many cases it is a matter of having a fundamentally different ecclesiology and Christology. But they are sensitive issues. When Jesus promised his Spirit to his disciples, he made it clear: "When the Spirit of truth comes, he will guide you into the whole truth (*pasa aletheia*) (Jn 16:13). Truth is not a collection of many truths; it is something whole and ultimately it is identified with God. What we have is a participation of it, imperfect and defective, seeing as in a mirror, dimly (1 Cor 13:12). But there is always a tendency to identify the part with the whole, and claim that one possesses the whole truth. Rather than being certain about having the full truth about a particular issue, some critical theologians claim that one is certain it is impossible ever to have the full truth about something expressed by one person or group. Here we have the beginning of prophetic confrontation.

The decisive factor in all prophetic involvement seems to be an ecumenical vision of things and issues, through which all issues related to humanity and the cosmos are understood as the concerns of theological reflection and praxis. Although ecumenism as a theological discipline grew up in the Church as an inter-Church issue in the context of the many divisions in the Church, today ecumenism is understood more as an approach to things from a wider and cosmic perspective, faithful to the inner meaning of the Greek word *oikoumene* as the inhabited earth. Ecumenism is essentially a cosmic vision. It has intra-Church, inter-Church, inter-religious, intra-humanity and intra-cosmic concerns. Ecumenism is hope in action, hope that the Church will be one, hope that the world will be one, hope that the obscurities of our life in this world would be clarified and its frustrations overcome when we see Jesus Christ, the crucified and risen one, as the hidden dynamism of history. What the *Declaration Toward a Global Ethic* promulgated by the Parliament of World's Religion in Chicago in 1993 should serve as a model and pattern for the world theologians to reflect on, to discuss and motivate the religions and the society to move into action.²

Towards the end of the Babylonian captivity Deutero-Isaiah exhorted Israel who had by then developed an introvert psychology of closing their doors to all other issues and concentrating only on their own petty interests: "Widen the space of your tent, extend the curtains of your home. Do not hold back! Lengthen your ropes, make your tent-pegs firm, for you will burst out to right and to left" (Is 54:2-3). This exhortation is very much applicable to the theologians and exegetes of our times who are also challenged to go out of their centripetal world of theological reflection to the wider world of God. In a global village of ours, it is but natural that the world of theologians and exegetes comes closer and shares their concerns and problems which will add beauty and meaning for their common theological ministry. In fact, it is heartening to see more and more theologians from the West opening themselves to the wider reality of the world, which presents them with issues which they never new about, such as the challenge of religious pluralism and the problem of poverty and misery facing the vast number of the human community. It is also important that the theologians in the so-called Third World also learn the discipline of critical thinking, hard word and research in theological reflection and academic life. Whether in the First World or in the Third World, the ultimate cause which theologians have to take care of is the cause of the Church and of the humankind at large.

What Karl Barth as a theologian of the Word of God has contributed towards a dialectical theology during the 20th century, what Dietrich Bonhoeffer has persuasively established through his nonreligious interpretation of the Bible and through his message of Christian worldliness, what Karl Rahner has convincingly developed in his doctrine of theological anthropology and the complementary understanding of nature and grace, what the scientist-philosopher-theologian Teilhard de Chardin arrived at through his innovative theological conclusions about *cosmogenesis* and a theology of optimism and hope within the context of a coherence of the sacred and the secular, and what Hans Küng has painstakingly established through his ever-widening ecumenism from inter-Church through inter-religious to intra-cosmic are all prophetic contributions which we have to share and develop to make the Church and her theology relevant and meaningful. What M.A. Thomas in the Indian Church did through his total ecumenical vision and what M. M. Thomas in the Indian Subcontinent achieved through his integrated vision of the unity of the temporal and the spiritual order and through his struggle for the humanization of the self

---

² Cf. Hans Küng-Karl-Josef Kuschel (Eds), *A Global Ethic. The Declaration of the Parliament of the World's Religions* (London: SCM Press, 1993).

and the society, sometimes as a dissenter and rebel, often crossing established borders and barriers, and what D. S. Amalorpadass contributed through his relentless efforts to make the Church truly and authentically Indian through his courageous efforts of inculturation and other challenging programmes should always remain as a source of inspiration for the younger generation of prophetic persons in the Indian Church.

IV

MISSION OF THE CHURCH IN THE WORLD

On March 12, 2000 something very unusual and, at the same time, inspiring took place in St. Peter's Square, Rome. Pope John Paul II, the head of the one billion Roman Catholics belonging to 22 *sui juris* Churches, made a public apology and a request for pardon from all those concerned, for the seven capital offenses committed by the Catholic Church during the past several centuries. These offenses touch almost all areas of the Church's presence and action in history during the past several centuries, such as, disunity among Christians, forced conversions, hatred towards other religions, Inquisition, anti-semitism, negative attitude towards minorities and women, and defects in the attitude of the Church towards human rights taken as a whole. The reaction of the world to this gesture of the Pope was mixed. Some hailed it as a noble and sacred act of a Church that is conscious and aware of its limitations. Others found it unnecessary for the Church to humiliate itself before the world. Still others found the whole thing as irrelevant and meaningless for the simple reason that, what has happened in the past, has already happened and there is no point in recalling them and trying to mend for them. The present and future are more important than what has happened in the past. But all were convinced that it was the first of its kind in the history of the Church, especially in modern times.

Without going into a critique of this extraordinary event, it must be admitted that it was the best way for the Church to reveal to the world that it is still a Church of sinners, that it is still very human, and that it is not all holy and blameless and without wrinkles, as was the customary language in the past. Ever since Martin Luther ventured on a reformation of the Church from within, the expression that "the Church is in need of a reformation" was considered as a heretical formula till Vatican II indirectly approved of it as a valid and healthy approach to the Church involved in a pilgrimage through history. It means that the Church is basically a pilgrim Church in history. Understood in this manner, what the Pope did was a genuine expression of the Church's self-awareness and its readiness to reform itself, to undo the wrongs of her past. It was a bold attempt to admit the fact that the Church is still the servant in the world and not its master, trying to carry out her duties; but at times also making mistakes and deviating from her true mission. It was also an invitation to all the members of the Roman Catholic Church to develop a culture of reconciliation and not one of confrontation with the world. Thereby the Pope was trying to heal the wounds of the past and make the Church an instrument of peace and joy in the world. Only people with a prophetic sense of history can dare do such great things.

Ever since the historic event of Vatican II, the Roman Catholic Church has become very much conscious of, and more and more committed to its pastoral mission in the world. Almost all the 16 documents of Vatican II endorse this pastoral vision and dimension of the ministry of the Church in a clear manner. The most significant document among these is the Pastoral Constitution on the Church in the World. The importance of this document lies not only in the fact that it enjoys the unique distinction of it being the only major document to have originated directly from a suggestion made on the floor of the Council's Aula itself, but also because it ranks high as the most characteristic achievement of an essentially 'pastoral council', the first of its kind in the history of the Roman Catholic Church. After having theologically explained the inner nature of the Church in *Lumen Gentium*, with its various categories of membership, this document refers to the mission of the Church in the world. The two words through which this document is introduced, *Gaudium (joy) et Spes (hope),* lay emphasis on the positive attitude the Church has towards her mission in the world, namely, joy for being in the world as well as hope about the world. The Church is now more aware of the message of John 3:16 about God loving the world than the out-of-the-context interpretation of 1 John 2:15-17 about the hatred towards the world. The world is no more considered as the enemy of the Church. What James in his letter (4:4) wrote about the mistake of 'friendship with the world' is to be understood in its specific historical and social context of a Christian life devoid of inner substance and commitment to praxis. After centuries of exclusive preoccupation with the inner nature of the Church regarding its structure and hierarchical details, the Church has at last become very much conscious of its mission in the world and this awareness has inaugurated a new era of pastoral concern and commitment in the Church as a whole and in all the sections of the people of God. The traditional understanding of the triple ministry of the Church in terms of 'preaching and teaching', 'sanctifying' and 'governing' has now taken on a new formulation through which 'governing' has been replaced by 'serving' and 'shepherding'. All members of the Church have to take up the role of servants and shepherds in the world, and thereby they have to assume the role Jesus took upon himself as the one who came to serve and give his life as a ransom for the world (Mk 10:45). This new formulation of the concept of 'service' with its accent on personalism has restored the New Testament message of involvement and availability as the hallmark of the Church.

The Church in the Vision of Christ

In the Greek world the term *ekklesia* meant a group of citizens "called out" to assemble for legislative or deliberative politcal purposes.[1] This assembly included only the citizens who enjoyed full rights, and thus the word implies the dignity of the members and the legality of the assembly. As a whole this word had no religious usage. This secular meaning of *ekklesia* is found in Acts 19:32,39,41, where it is used in the sense of a gathering of people. The Greek translation of the Old Testament (LXX) adopted *ekklesia* to translate the Hebrew word *qahal*, which, with the other Hebrew word *edah,* signifies in later Hebrew the religious assembly of the Israelites. Deut 23:1-3 use *qehal Yahweh* as referring to the community of the people of Israel. In course of time, these two Hebrew words were adopted for the local religious assembly of the Jews who lived outside of Jerusalem, and *edah* was more commonly rendered in Greek by *synagoge*, the word from which the English word 'synagogu' is derived. Since the Jews during the first century used *synagoge* as referring to their religious gatherings, the first Greek-speaking Christians selected the word *ekklesia* to show that their roots lay in the OT and that they continued to be the OT people of God in a new manner. The Lucan story of Stephen in the Acts also suggests this Old Testament origin of the word, where Stephen is made to refer to the Israel of old as *he ekklesia en te eremo*, meaning the congregation of Israel in the desert (Acts 7:38 with a reference to Dt 4:10).

Looking at the reality of the Church as it exists today and reflecting on what made the Church to become so complex a reality, some people, even well-meaning people, are tempted to ask a question: "Did Jesus Christ ever intend to found a Church?" It is a question that has far-reaching consequences for historians and theologians. It is true that there is only passage in the Gospels, where Jesus is explicitly said to have founded the Church during his earthly ministry (Matt 6:16-18). But it is the considered view of many biblical scholars that this is basically a story of the post-resurrection tradition, now projected into the past, something similar to John 21:15-17 about Jesus, after his resurrection, entrusting the care of his present and future disciples to a rehabilitated Peter. Whereas the Matthean tradition emphasizes the faith dimension of the future community, the Johannine tradition lays emphasis on love with its vertical and horizontal dimensions as the hallmark of the Church. Even though the term

---

[1] The Anglo-Saxon group of words (English *church*, Scotish *kirk*, German *Kirche*, Dutch *kerk*) are derived from the late Greek word *kyriakon* meaning "of the Lord" referring to the *hemera kyriake* translated as "Lord's Day", a day on which the early Christians assembled to celebrate the Lord's Supper.

ecclesia is seldom found in the Gospels, the beginnings of the reality of the Church are already found in the Gospels through many images. Jesus preached the nearness of the kingdom of God (Mk 1:1-15) and in view of its coming and growth in the world he formed a group of disciples and followers. Of these disciples he demanded a personal commitment through which they would understand the meaning of his mission and thereby continue to preach the Good News of the kingdom of God, once his earthly ministry was completed, thereby inviting people to accept the message of the kingdom of God (Mk 3:13-15). It is probable that this preparation for the future mission of the disciples as an organized community legitimized the inclusion of the primacy passage of Matt 16:16-19 inserted as a pre-resurrection story. The theological and kerygmatic influence of this ecclesial passage can be found also in Matt 18:1-35 where Jesus gives his directives to those who were to be leaders in the community, how they had to respect and take care of the simple members of the community and guide them when they went wrong. Moreover, the leaders were reminded that the risen Lord is ever present in the community, and that all their actions regarding others should be undertaken with that awareness of his presence in the community (Matt 18:20). Consequently, they were instructed to forgive others willingly and create a community of reconciled members (Matt 18:23-35).

In 1971 C. H. Dodd, who was considered as a very prominent and a balanced theologian and biblical scholar, wrote the book *The Founder of Christianity*, for which he was awarded a prize by the Queen of England. It is a work known for its scholarship and simplicity and it pays to read it with amazing delight to discover in its pages the portrait of a person who changed the course of history. But reflecting on the very title of this book, *The Founder of Christianity,* it is felt that this is precisely what Jesus of Nazareth was not. He is not the founder of Christianity in the ordinary sense of the term. What Jesus did was to start a movement in religion and not a religion itself, and he wanted that this dynamism of a movement should always be kept up. The expression 'Christianity' is not found in the New Testament. The disciples of Jesus at Antioch were called "Christians"; but it was more as a nickname than as a designation. There are only two words in the Greek New Testament which refer to what could be designated as 'Christianity'. They are *he hodos*, used several times in the Acts of the Apostles, meaning *the Way* and *adelphotes*, found only once in 1 Peter 5:9, referring to the quality of relationship between the members of this movement as brothers and sisters. It is precisely this dynamic reality of the way of life, characterized by personal relationship, that in course of time came to be known as 'Christianity'. Its real history began with the conversion of the Roman Emperor, Constantine the Great, from whose time onwards

Christianity became a parallel reality to the Roman Empire under the protection and control of the Roman Emperor. It is everybody's knowledge how the Church from that time onwards departed from the authentic parameters of the New Testament Church. The later history of the Church was characterized by a series of power politics, ongoing divisions in the Church, the Crusades, the Inquisition, Church-assisted Colonialism, which were all making the Church more and more alienated and estranged from its true mission.

The earliest usage of the word *ekklesia* in the New Testament reflects the idea of the religious assembly of the believers, taken as a whole and also their local assembly. The title is first applied to the Church of Jerusalem, which was itself a local community. It was, at the same time, the assembly of all who believed in Jesus Christ, and thus was the legitimate successor of the Israelite assembly of Yahweh. In its initial phases the Church of Jerusalem was not clearly aware of its distinction from Judaism. Its members were accustomed to meet and to pray in the temple of Jerusalem and they regarded themselves as in every way faithful to the Mosaic Law and the practices of Judaism. The question of the relationship between the Church and Judaism did not become acute until Gentiles were admitted to the Church in large numbers and finally formed separate local Churches in other places, of which the earliest and the largest was the Church of Antioch. It then became necessary for the Church to identify itself as a community distinct from Judaism, into which Gentiles could be admitted to full standing without becoming Jews and undertaking the obligations of the Jewish law.

The Church in the Acts of the Apostles

The term 'Church' occurs in none of the early chapters of the Acts and when it first appears in 5:11, it is found in the comment with which Luke concludes his account of Ananias and Saphira incident: "Great fear fell upon the whole Church". Here Luke is using the name current in his own day to designate the early Jerusalem Christian community, the nature of which he had summarized in 2:42-47 and 4:32-35. In these passages Luke explains the life-style of the community as characterized by the teaching of the apostles, community of goods, unity in mind and heart, prayer in the temple of Jerusalem and the breaking of bread. The name *ekklesia* first appears with the beginning of the story of Paul and the great persecution against the Church in Jerusalem (8:1). From then on the name *Church* occurs 29 times in the Acts. It is used not only of the Christian community of Jerusalem (8:3; 11:22; 12:1,5; 15:4,22; 18:22), but also of that in Antioch (11:26; 13:1; 14:27; 15:3), in Lystra and Iconium (14:23), in Syria and Cilicia (15:41), in Ephesus (20:17,28), in unnamed cities (16:4), and throughout all Judea, Galilee and

Samaria (9:31). Thereby Luke made the concept of the Church applicable to all authentic communities in various parts of the Roman Empire.

What is more important to note about the reality of the Church in the Acts is the way in which the Church grew up in its early stages and established its identity as something different from Judaism. Though Jesus of Nazareth had envisaged the community of his followers as an entirely new one consisting of all humans qualified by their conversion (*metanoia*) and faith (Mk 1:14-15), the community in Jerusalem had almost identified itself as a new sect of Judaism (Acts 24:5) which accepted Jesus of Nazareth as its Messiah. In all other matters its members wanted to remain within the framework of Judaism and its practices. The first person to question this identification was Stephen, one of the seven "servants of the table" (Acts 6:1-6), elected by the community and authorized by the apostles to take care of the distribution of food when the Hellenistic widows were being neglected by the Palestinian Jewish Christians. Stephen realized that this tension between the Palestinian and Hellenistic Jewish Christians was basically a question related to the understanding of the very identity of the Christian movement as was preached by Jesus of Nazareth (6:8-8:1a).[2]

A very important aspect of the Church we have to keep in mind is that the early Church grew up through the crises it underwent, crises that were created by certain authentic persons and approved by the Spirit of God. The most important among these critical leaders were Stephen, Philip and Paul. It was through them that the original plan of the risen Lord, summarized in Acts 1:8, was realized. Whereas Stephen, full of the Spirit, questioned the claim of absolutism maintained by Judaism, which led to the persecution of the Jerusalem Church and the dispersion of the disciples of Jesus, Philip went to Samaria and preached to the Samaritans, making it possible for them to accept the gospel. We read in the Acts that Peter and John went to Samaria and approved the mission of Philip (8:14-17). The persecution believers in Christ, mentioned above, also resulted in some of these disciples going as far as Antioch and founding the first Church among the Gentiles (11:19-26), which later became the important centre of missionary dynamism among the Gentiles (13:1-3). The call Paul received from the risen Christ to stop persecuting the disciples of Christ and his consequent commitment to the gospel of Christ, taking it to the entire Roman Empire, was the most significant event in the history of the early Church. This event, together with the later story of Peter, being

---

[2] Cf. Joseph Pathrapankal, "The Church in the Acts of the Apostles: A model for our times" *ThD* 34(1987)19-24.

compelled by God to accept the Gentile Cornelius into the community of the believers in Christ (10:1-11:18), forms the backdrop of the later expansion of the Church in the wide Gentile world, initiated by the Church of Antioch through the mission of Paul and Barnabas (13:1-3).

The mission of Paul and Barnabas was very successful. Although their first target was to preach to the Hellenistic Jews, it proved that they were not prepared to accept the gospel and so they turned to the Gentiles, and they were glad to accept the gospel (13:44-52). But this mission among the Gentiles and their joining the community of the believers created a new problem. Many Jewish Christians were of the view that the Gentile Christians should undergo the Jewish rite of circumcision and observance of the Mosaic Law. Once Paul and Barnabas returned to Antioch after their first missionary journey, the problem became very acute. Some individuals from Judea came to Antioch and argued with the believers in Antioch that unless the Gentile Christians are circumcised according to the custom of Moses, they cannot be saved. The sectarian understanding of the Christian movement once again became strong. Luke's description of the Jerusalem Council in the Acts of the Apostles (15:3-12) tries to establish that the discussion held in it and the decisive intervention of Peter in this meeting finally solved the problem. Whereas in Acts 15:3-12 Luke narrates the story of the Council with its emphasis on Peter, the Pauline version of the same event in Gal 2:1-10 is about the decisive role played by Paul himself in solving the problem.[3] Although the question of circumcision was officially discussed and solved in the Jerusalem meeting, it continued to disturb the Gentile Christians in the Gentile Churches, such as in the Galatian territory and the Church of Philippi (Phil 3:2-3). On the whole, the author of the Acts tries to present the Church as something which grew up not in spite of the crises but because of the crises it had to undergo, precisely because it was guided by the Spirit of God and Spirit-guided persons.

The Pauline understanding of the Church

One of the richest contributions Paul has made to Christian theology is his profound reflection on the Church, which he undertook not as an abstract

---

[3] Acts 15:13-29 seems to be the description of a later event presided over by James regarding the table fellowship of Jewish and Gentile Christians, for which several conditions were given to the Gentile Christians to suit the Jewish customs. A letter was sent to Antioch that contained the decisions of this meeting. Paul came to know about this meeting only when he returned to Jerusalem after his third missionary journey (21:25). Paul, as such, did not seem to have respected the contents of this letter (cf. 1 Cor 10:27-29; Gal 2:11-12; Col 2:21-22).

speculation but as something which resulted from his own personal experience, right from the beginning of his commitment to Christ.[4] In the question of the Risen Lord to Saul: "Why do you persecute me?" and in his answer: "I am Jesus whom you are persecuting" (cf. Acts 9:4-5; 22:7-8; 26:14-15), we may see the seed of Paul's later understanding of Christ in relation to the Church, namely, the close relationship between Christ and the believers who constitute the Church.

a) Paul and the Jerusalem Church

Through his conversion Paul came into close contact with the Jerusalem Church, which he calls the "Church of God" (Gal 1:13). He realized that this Church was the authorized community of the risen Lord. It was here that on the day of Pentecost God once again gathered together the dispersed tribes of Israel and constituted the new *qehal Yahweh*, and the uniqueness and inalienable position of this Church Paul was always prepared to recognize.[5] Later on the same title Paul attributed to the other Churches in Judea, when he tells the Thessalonians that they have become imitators of the Churches of God which are in Judea (cf. 1 Thes 2:14; 2 Thes 1:4; Gal 1:22; 1 Cor 11:16; 1 Cor 14:33). Paul always maintained an attitude of respect and concern for the Church of Jerusalem and the other Churches in Judea in matters of tradition and customs. He went to Jerusalem to present to the leaders there the gospel which he preached among the Gentiles lest somehow he should be running or had run in vain (Gal 2:2). He organized a collection of money in many parts of Asia Minor and Greece to help the poor Christians of Judea at the request of the leaders of the Jerusalem Church.[6] Paul even considered it an obligation on

---

[4] On this topic there are several specialized studies: L.Cerfaux, *The Church in the theology of St.Paul* (New York: Herder and Herder, 1958); R.Schnackenburg, *The Church in the New Testament*,(London: Burns and Oates, 1965); J.Pathrapankal, "Pauline Theology of the Church" *Jeevadhara* 15(1985)148-158.

[5] Cf. L.Cerfaux *op.cit.* pp.106-117. According to Gal 1:18 Paul went to Jerusalem to visit Cephas apparently to consult him about the content of the gospel he had to preach.

[6] It has been argued sometimes that the collection which Paul organized for the poor Christians of the Jerusalem Church was more a diplomatic action to please the authorities of that Church who were rather critical of his attitude towards the Torah. It is true that through this gesture he was aiming at something "honourable not only in the Lord's sight but also in the sight of men" (2 Cor 8:21). But his main purpose was to help the poor in their basic needs, recalling the example of Christ (2 Cor 8:9). If he were to be pleasing men, he would not have become the servant of Christ (Gal 1:10). In fact, the Jerusalem authorities had requested Paul "to remember the poor" and Paul writes that he had been only eager to do it (Gal 2:10). On the comprehensive meaning of Gal 2:10 see J.Pathrapankal, "Apostolic commitment and "remembering the poor", A study in Gal 2:10" in *Texts and Contexts* ed. by T.Fornberg and D.Hellholm (Oslo, Scandinavian University Press, 1995)pp.1001-1018.

the part of the Gentile Churches to do it as a mark of respect in return for the many spiritual blessings the Gentile Churches had received from the mother Church of Jerusalem (Rom 15:27-28).

b) The Church of the Jews and Gentiles

Paul's mission from Antioch to the Gentiles (13:1-14:28) and the founding of several Churches in Asia Minor, and later on in Greece brought him face to face with a new challenge in his understanding of the Church as a whole. It was a question of relating all these churches to the Jerusalem Church. The Council of Jerusalem brought home to him, on the one hand, the significance of the Church of Jerusalem, and on the other hand, the fundamental truth that faith in Jesus Christ was the decisive criterion for anyone to become a disciple of Christ and belong to the Church. The fact that this decision was taken in the Jerusalem Church meant, for Paul, the recognition of a new approach to the reality of the Church (Acts 15:3-12; Gal 2:1-10). As a result of this new insight into the mystery of the Church Paul began to develop a practical theology of the Church. In Phil 4:15 the community of Philippi is specified as an *ekklesia* in the full sense of the word, which came forward to help Paul in his personal needs, and the letter is addressed to the "saints, bishops and the deacons at Philippi" (Phil 1:1).

As we have explained above, in his early letters Paul still gives the title "Church of God" or "Churches of God" to the Jerusalem Church or to Churches in Judea. But his encounter with the community at Corinth gave him the insight to realize the need of recognizing the full ecclesial aspect of such local communities also, not in opposition to the Jerusalem Church but as a natural outcome of his theological reflection about the Church in God's plan of salvation. Paul's first attempt was to give the title "Church of God" (*ekklesia tou theou*) to the Church of the Corinthians (1 Cor 1:1; 2 Cor 1:1). It was a bold step taken by Paul to see the Gentile Church of Corinth also as a "Church of God". So he was trying to bring about order and discipline in the Corinthian Church with a reference to the customs and traditions in the Church of God in Judea (cf. 1 Cor 11:2,16). For Paul it was not a question of an independent, but of an inter-dependent growth of the various Churches. One of the chief reasons why the Church in the first century of the Common Era, which was rapidly growing in its extent, did not split up is to be found in Paul's theological and practical approach which made all the believers vividly conscious of the unity conferred on them by God which imperatively called for concord and cooperation among them. For Paul, the Church was not merely the loose association of those who believed in Christ, but rather there was an organic unity which should characterize the relationship between the various Churches.

An important idea which Paul developed with regard to the reality of the Church is his concept of the Church as the Body of Christ. Whatever be the origin of the expression `body' (*soma*) as related to a community,[7] for Paul, it is related to the Eucharistic Body of Christ which constituted the basis of his understanding of the Church as the body of Christ: Because there is one Bread, we who are many are one body, for we partake of the one bread" (1 Cor 10:17). The Eucharistic Body is the point of departure as well as the point of convergence for the Church as the Body of Christ. At the same time, the Eucharist is the intensified articulation of the Body of Christ that is already constituted by baptism into Christ: "By one Spirit we were all baptized into one Body - Jews or Greeks, slaves or free - and all were made to drink of the one Spirit" (1 Cor 12:13). It is from this basic concept of the Body that Paul later evolved the understanding of the cosmic Church as related to the cosmic Christ.

d) The Church in the Captivity Letters

After considering these specific meanings the concept of the Church has in the Pauline writings, we now look at a new approach of Paul to the reality of the Church. In his letters to the Colossians and Ephesians,[8] the Church is presented as belonging to the very plan of God. In Eph 1:3-10 Paul explains how the Father has planned the entire historical process of salvation from a perspective with its beginning, centre and goal in the person of Christ, in whom both the Jews (Eph 1:11-12) and the Gentiles (Eph 2:13-14) have been brought together. In Eph 1:15-23 Paul explains how the Father has put all things under Christ and has made him the head (*kephale*) over all things for the sake of the Church, which is his body as well as the fullness (*pleroma*) of him who fills all in all. For Paul, the Church is a reality constituted by the coming together of the *laos* and *ethne* in the person and through the work of Christ. Paul explains it at length in Eph 2:11-22. The Church is basically the Church of the Jews and Gentiles, and all those factors which so far created divisions among them are now abolished for ever. Paul says that Christ in his person has broken down the dividing wall of hostility between these two opposing groups and has reconciled both of them creating a new humanity (*kainos anthropos*) out of them (Eph 2:15), and bringing them together into the one body of the Church so that all can have access to the Father in one Spirit. In Paul's cosmic

---

[7] The antecedents of the Pauline conception of body are not obvious and a number of suggestions have been made: Stoicism, Gnosticism, Rabbinic speculation on the cosmic body of Adam, the OT idea of corporate personality and the Eucharist.

[8] Here We do not enter into a discussion of the Pauline authorship of these two letters.

view Christ is the head of the Church, which is his body, and he is thereby the head of all creation. The Church is thus equated with the fullness of Christ and is given cosmic dimensions. Paul praises the Father for his wisdom "through the Church and through Christ Jesus" (Eph 3:21). "Here there cannot be Greek and Jew, circumcised and uncircumcised, barbarian, Scythian, slave, free man, but Christ is all, and in all (*panta en pasin Christos*) (Col 3:11). Here we have the principle of unity and diversity brought into a harmony, and we owe this important concept of the Church to the rich theological insight of Paul

Since the Church belongs to God's plan of salvation, all the members of the Church have to work together to maintain unity and at the same time foster growth. Because there is only one body, it is necessary that all factors which favour unity are to be brought together in order to safeguard the unity of the body: one spirit, one Lord, one faith, one baptism, one God the Father and the one hope that is common to all. But this unity is not a passive and static one; rather it is a dynamic one which should enable all the members of the Church to grow into mature persons, measuring up to the maturity of Christ himself (Eph 4:1-16). The charisms shared by the members of the Church should be made use of for building up the body of Christ (Eph 4:12) till all attain to the unity of the faith and of the knowledge of the Son of God (cf. Eph 4:13).

The question naturally arises: "Where is this Church to be found?" It does not seem that Paul identified this Church with any historical manifestation of it in time and space. What he was trying to establish was that all historical articulations of the Church are feeble and imperfect manifestations of this cosmic and transcendent reality. Paul never tried to exhaust the meaning of the word 'Church' with any of its historical articulations. In fact, it was his experience with several historical manifestations of the Church with their own specific characteristics that prompted Paul to have a transcendent approach to the reality of the Church and he realized that only so could he establish a relationship between Christ and the Church. As Paul once stopped considering Christ from a human point of view (2 Cor 5:16) in order to see his real greatness and universal role, so, too, he stopped considering every historical manifestation of the Church as a relative one, whether it be the Church of Jerusalem or the Church of Antioch, in order to have a clearer vision of the role and meaning of the Church as a cosmic and transcendent reality in God's plan of salvation, namely, the Church as a gathering together of all peoples and nations beyond all structural and juridical specifications.

In this transcendental dimension the Church manifests several characteristics. First of all, the Church begins to reveal itself as a mystery. The visible expressions of the Church do not in any way remove its mystery aspects. In so far as the Church is the "new humanity" (*kainos anthropos*) (Eph 2:15) consisting of Jews and Gentiles and is the "body of Christ" and the "bride of Christ" (Eph 5:22-23), it is also a mystery. The Church is a mystery because it has a heavenly dimension and the members of the Church have their citizenship also in heaven (Phil 3:20). In this sense the Church becomes ultimately a heavenly reality, already removed from this passing world (*aion*) and is relate to Christ, the head of the body. It is the sphere of the rule of the heavenly and exalted Christ, enthroned with God (Col 1:13). The Dogmatic Constitution on the Church (*Lumen Gentium*) of Vatican II has established this basic fact as of vital importance in our understanding of the Church. To understand the Church as a mystery means to lift the discussion about the Church above the level of its historical manifestations and institutional organization. To speak of the Church as a mystery is to confess God's constant sovereignty over all things. It also implies that the whole Church is mysteriously present in each local Church, but that no Church, however numerous, organized and powerful, exhausts the fullness of the Church. After dealing with the reality of the Church from the moment of his new commitment to Christ throughout the decisive years of the growth and expansion of the gospel in Judea, Samaria, Syria, Asia Minor, Greece, and Rome it is this conviction that Paul arrived at. It is also the perspective within which Catholic ecclesiology is to be understood and presented in our times, especially because of its inherent claim to absolutism and uniqueness. However, this transcendent aspect of the Church does not it any way obliterate the need of an earthly and social dimension of it. In fact, these two dimensions are complementary and each in its own way contributes to the richness of the reality of the Church. This emphasis on the transcendent and heavenly aspect of the Church could be seen as a corrective to understanding the Church as a mere earthly, human reality, a danger the Church has always to be aware of. During the middle ages this truth was not yet recognized and the following several centuries witnessed a Church which was trying to imitate secular organizations.

c) House-Churches in the Pauline Letters

A unique contribution of Paul to the theology of Church is his frequent reference to `House-Church' (*he kat'oikon ekklesia*)[9] in his letters, thereby meaning a Church operating in the household of Christians.[10]

---

[9] The Greek expression can be translated as: "The Church constituted according to household" or "Church in the household".

[10] This expression occurs four times in the letters of Paul: 1 Cor 16:19; Rom 16:3-5; Philm 1-2; Col 4:15.

This approach to the reality of the Church emphasized the important fact that the Church is primarily a community of people without any aspect of it being a structure or institution. We do not know much about the sociological background of this phenomenon, namely, whether it was patterned on the Synagogue gatherings of the Hellenistic Jews.[11] It is probable that such gatherings were necessitated by the fact that Christianity was not yet a recognized religion in the Roman Empire. Consequently the gathering in private houses became a practical need. However, such gatherings gave a new dimension to the reality of the Church in so far as such local gatherings were also called `Churches'. Thus we have the reference to the "house Church of Aquila and Prisca" (1 Cor 16:19; Rom 16:3-5a), and the "house Church of Nympha" (Col 4:15). In Acts 2:46 we read that the believers were breaking bread in their homes (*kat'oikon*). It seems the `house Church' offered a natural context for the Eucharistic celebration as an expression Christian love and fellowship that was violated in the Church of Corinth (1 Cor 11:17-22). The phenomenon of the `house Church' provided the early Christians with a concrete experience of understanding the dynamic nature of the Church. Though this system gradually disappeared in course of time, the message it brings has some relevance in our times in so far as families are to be understood as the most natural and concrete manifestations of a living and dynamic Church.[12]

What Paul had established as the inner dynamism and the spiritual reality of the Church was practically lost sight of during the colonial times. Local cultures were wiped out, all religions except Christianity were understood as works of the devil, and becoming members of the Church was presented as indispensable for salvation, for which intense missionary work was organized throughout the world. It took us towards the middle of the 20th century to evolve a new awareness in the Churches about their new role in human history and in the world. For many Churches in the Orthodox traditions and the Protestant traditions, it resulted in the formation of the World Council of Churches which began to evolve new attitudes to the wider realities of the world, such as world

---

[11] On the subject of "house-church" cf. H.Josef Klauck, *Hausgemeinde und Hauskirche in frühen Christentum (SBS, 103)*, Stutgart,1981; N.Povenchen, "The family as domestic church" *Theology Digest*, 30(1982) 149-152; H.-J Klauck, "The house-church as a way of life" *Theology Digest* 30(1982)153-157; F.V.Wilson, "The Significance of the early house Churches" *JBL* 58(1939) 110-114; R.Banks, *Paul's idea of community: The early house churches in their historical setting*, Grand Rapids, 1980.

[12] *Lumen Gentium* (art 11) speaks of the family as the most significant unit of the Church. The Fifth General Assembly of the Synod of Bishops held in 1980 had the theme: "The duties of the Christian family in the contemporary world."

religions, questions of human rights, and issues of justice and peace. For the Roman Catholic Church it was the Second Vatican Council which made it aware of the larger issues of the world, to which the 16 documents of this Council addressed and responded in a meaningful manner. Hence the present-day Christians are privileged to live during these blessed times and, though it is difficult to forget the past, the best way to face the present and the future is to learn from the past in such a way that they do not repeat the past. The most important lesson the Churches have to learn in our times is to become aware of the fact that the Church now exists in a pluralistic world and consequently it has to respond to the issues of this pluralistic world.

Church in the Book of Revelation

A concluding reflection on the New Testament Church is the Church in the book of Revelation with its two aspects of being a Church in the process of decadence and also a persecuted Church struggling to survive in the Roman Empire. The early chapters of this book devote their attention to inviting the seven Churches of Asia Minor to a radical conversion because they have abandoned their first love for Christ. Hence there is a passionate call for a radical conversion and a re-establishing of the original commitment to Christ (Rev 2:1-3:22). Together with it, we have also the painful picture of a Church which is being persecuted, and the task of the author is to comfort, console and encourage the Church to face these persecutions as part of their Christian call. The most consoling dimension of this exhortation is that there will be an end to these persecutions and a new age will be inaugurated through the dawn of a new heaven and a new earth (Rev 21:1-4). What is significant in these discussions is the awareness that the Church is the "little flock" which is protected and taken care of by God. In our efforts to understand the meaning and role of the Church in our times, especially in the context of ecumenism, we should keep in mind this complex reality of the Church as it is presented in the New Testament. Any attempt to forget the historical background of the New Testament Church carries with it the danger of equating the present with the past and glossing over the important ideas related to the inner nature of this divine-human reality.

The Church and the Pluralistic World

The basic reality that characterizes the world of our times is that it is a pluralistic world. In fact, pluralism is the basic datum of contemporary thinking and living all over the world. Pluralism basically means the acceptance of the other as the *other* with all its uniqueness, not as something opposed to oneself, nor as an extension of oneself, but something with its own inalienable qualities and characteristics. Pluralism also denotes the concept of the one and the many, the one as something basic to all things, coordinating the many and the many as coordinated to the one, thereby creating harmony and peace among the many. Hence pluralism means difference and distinction; but it is not divisiveness, and a pluralistic world does not mean a divided world. Once pluralism is accepted as a basic reality of this world and its historical process at various levels, it becomes easier for all to see the legitimacy of the others to exist and operate at various levels of life and the positive role pluralism plays in enriching all. We are living in world rich in pluralism Our pluralistic world is characterized by a variety of issues, which can be summarized as follows: Ethnic pluralism, religious pluralism, scriptural pluralism, social pluralism, cultural pluralism, gender pluralism, ethical pluralism, political pluralism, ideological pluralism, linguistic pluralism, ecclesial pluralism and theological pluralism. It is this richness of pluralism which reveals the beauty of our human community as a whole, because God has created a world characterized all through by its own pluralism at various levels. It is this variety and pluralism that gives beauty to the environment in which we live.

In our times, throughout the world, there is a growing awareness of the need of accepting and respecting this pluralism, although it brings in its train a series of issues and problems at the religious, social, economic and political levels. We have to recognize the impact of philosophical and theological reflection characteristic of all religions in shaping and promoting this pluralistic awareness. It is universally experienced that the world has undergone more changes during the past 50 years than it witnessed during the past 500 years and more. Our world is now characterized by a lot of mobility. There are mass movements of peoples going from one country to another in search of work or fleeing from war and other related problems. Education has also become internationalized with students moving from one continent to another. Tourism has opened up all five continents to people to see, learn and enjoy life. As a result of all these developments religions also have opened their doors to all peoples. Never before has so much of information been available regarding the ways in which different peoples of the world think, live and work. All these developments have created their own blessings and burdens. But all have to accept this new situation whether they like it or not. Hence the Church also must be ready to accept this reality of the pluralistic world.

World religions as well as various nations of the world are beginning to experience that their progress and growth do not any more consist in isolation, but rather in openness to other religions and other nations and their cultures. Those who are involved in religions and politics are also becoming more and more convinced that any attempt to dominate and monopolize in the realm of religion or politics is self-defeating. There is no more question of any religious or political or cultural or any other absolutes. Equally excluded is the tendency to establish one's own religion or culture as something normative for the whole humankind. With all these new developments what has happened is the creation and evolution of a global village, in which all have to live in relationship and sharing. Pluralistic thinking in the understanding of the meaning and role of religions is one of the crucial issues affecting the humankind in our times. Religious pluralism also affects the Church's self-understanding and her mission. Traditionally known as a Christian country, Europe is now realizing that here the Christians have to live together with the followers of other religions, millions of whom are now living in these countries, so much so that they have also to make extra arrangements to the children of these religious traditions their own respective faiths in the class rooms. In the Asian countries the situation is very different. There the Christians have to live and work in the midst of other religions. In the sub-continent of India there are practically all the major religions of the world. All these phenomena necessitate a great deal of re-thinking and re-appraisal on the part of the Christians who have so far been trained to understand their religion in terms of uniqueness, exclusivism and superiority over other religions, and it is now psychologically not easy for them to change their attitudes. But a re-thinking is absolutely necessary. They have to undo the wrongs of the past and build up a new future.

If we look at the early history of the Church, it is clear that the broad outlook of some of the Fathers of the Church about Christianity was gradually rejected through the interventions of some interested theologians during the following centuries. We have the sublime teaching of several Fathers of the Church, such as Irenaeus and Justin, who taught that the eternal Logos was present and active in every human heart even before Christ was born. All those who followed their inner guidance, their genuine conscience, could arrive at salvation. Justin even said that all who live according to the Logos are basically Christians. But once Christianity became the official religion of the Roman Empire, this broad outlook on the followers of other religions was completely changed. "No salvation outside the Church" became the standard doctrine of the Church. Consequently, many steps were taken to make people in other parts of the world enter the Church as the only way left for them to arrive at salvation. Hence colonialism and missionary propaganda went hand in hand. Mission was understood as the expansion of Christianity from the West. Christianity assumed an attitude that there was nothing beyond it, that it could control everything, that it can judge all issues in the world, religious and political.

But radical changes started taking place during the second half of the 20th century. It looks really strange that it took so many centuries for the Church to go back to the inner essence of the gospel, which was wrongly interpreted and applied to suit the interests of some countries and their leaders. But times have changed and are fast changing. Vatican II is the concrete expression of this openness to pluralism in the Roman Catholic Church. Other Churches also show sublime signs of this openness to pluralism. It is of great significance that this atmosphere of sharing in a spirit of service opens a new opportunity for all Churches to speak a language of persuasion and inspiration rather domination to the whole world. If we look at the Bible, we can still see that this is precisely what the various books of the Bible invite us to do. The Old Testament, as a whole, tries to maintain a pluralistic dimension for its existence and mission among the various peoples of its time. It is in this sense that we have to understand the efforts made by the Old Testament writers to adopt and adapt the literary forms and thought-patterns from the neighbouring peoples, such as the creation and flood stories, the law codes from the Ancient Near East, the agricultural feasts from the Canaanites and the Wisdom literature form Babylon and Egypt. The Temple of Jerusalem designed by Phoenician architects was a bold adaptation of Phoenician culture. It is said that the sea in the Temple supported by twelve bulls (1 Kgs 7:23-26) reflected the fertility and mythological motifs of the Ancient Near East. A very challenging example of a pluralistic approach is the figure of a foreign king and priest, Melchizedeq, who blessed Abraham (Gen 14:17-20). Equally surprising is the boldness through which the author of the letter to the Hebrews presented Jesus Christ as a priest according to this Melchizedeq (Hb 7:1-28).

It is also important to see how in the midst of the efforts made by Ezra and the his followers to make Judaism an exclusivist religion there were also some reactions among the progressive Jewish thinkers who challenged the myopic and negative attitude of the mainstream Judaism. Two typical examples are the books of Ruth and Jonah. While the book of Ruth is a haggadic treatise appreciating the meaning of other religions besides Judaism, the book of Jonah is a prophetic satire, criticizing the official Judaism for its negative attitude towards other religions, represented through a pseudonymous prophet Jonah. Through these writings their authors tried to bring home to their fellow Jews that God has greater plans about other religions and that they should not stand in the way of God's ultimate plans. What is perhaps more remarkable is the courage and optimism shown by the leaders of Judaism who met in the Synod of Jamnia towards the end of the first century CE to finalize the canon of the Hebrew Scriptures. They accepted these books also as representing the faith of Israel, although the theology of these two books was very much different and almost opposed to the exclusivist attitude of the theology of the Deuteronimist tradition and that of Ezra and Nehemiah. Here we have a typical example of theological pluralism accepted into the canon of the Jewish Scriptures with its message and challenge for theological pluralism in our times.

Paul in the early Church also had to deal with several communities in matters of cultural practices which were unique to them. Some of these communities he had founded himself, others he was closely in touch with. In all of them Paul wanted to create an atmosphere of cultural freedom if it did not come into conflict with the basic principles of Christian faith and praxis. The Church of Rome was entirely different from the Church of Corinth or the Church of Philippi. He never wanted to apply his teaching to all of them in the same manner. Thus regarding the question of eating meat offered in the shrines of other religions Paul made a clear distinction between participating in the sacrifices of these religions and eating such meat or attending the social functions of the followers of other religions (1 Cor 10:25-27). Paul exhorted the Romans to obey the political authority like all other Romans (Rom 13:1-7) and he defended the personal freedom of each one regarding what they eat and regarding the observance of certain days which were all related to the customs and practices prevailing in the community of Rome during those days (Rom 14:1-6). The Church in our times also must be ready to adapt itself to the pluralistic world.

The Servant Church in a Pluralistic World

The time has come for the Church to recapture her role as the servant of the kingdom of God and build up her attitudes in accordance with the principles Jesus has envisaged for the Church. For this it is important that the Church assumes the role of the servant and nothing else. After having played a dominating role it is not easy for the Church to develop this servant attitude. But there is no other alternative to this radical demand in so far as the Church has to continue the mission of Christ who came to serve and not to be served (Mk 10:45). This is the new way of being the Church. This is a costly grace and costly discipleship, as D. Bonhoeffer has challengingly put it. The time is gone for the Church and other religions to sit together and discuss their dogmatic differences and come to some common agreement as if it is the goal of inter-religious relationship. The time is forever gone for one religion to teach others about what is right and what is wrong. There is nothing much that can be achieved in having some official documents about the positive attitudes religions must have towards each other. What is more imperative is the role religions together have to play in a pluralistic society of our times to guide it, to inspire it and also to challenge it. In other words, what is of utmost importance is the coming together of the world religions for a common programme of action to make the world a better place for people to live and work. Religions together must develop a new world vision and new style of inter-religious relationship. The followers of all religions must be characterized by religious authenticity, on the one hand, and religious complementarity, on the other hand. It is an ongoing process in which all religions have to engage themselves in all humility and courage. If God is the ultimate goal of all religions, he can be reached only through this process of transcendence, and all religions have to undergo a painful process of self-emptying, purification and transformation to arrive at this goal. The Church as the servant of the kingdom of God has to take a clear and pronounced leadership in this inter-religious cooperation.

We have explained above how the Church has to assume the attitude and role of the self-emptying servant of the kingdom of God in her presence and action in this pluralistic world. The question is not how big, powerful and influential the Church can become, but rather how it can remain the 'little flock' (Lk 12:32) and carry out her witnessing role with the power of the Holy Spirit. The mission command is not exhausted through what the risen Lord said at the end of Mathew's Gospel, nor does it seem that this should be the primary preoccupation of the Church, as it had been in the past: "Go and make disciples of all nations, baptizing them in the name of the Father and of the Son and of the Holy Spirit, teaching them to observe all that I have commanded you". He also said more emphatically: "You shall receive power when the Holy Spirit has come upon you; and you shall be my witnesses in Jerusalem and in all Judea and Samaria and to the end of the earth" (Acts 1:8). The abiding presence of the risen Lord promised to the disciples of Jesus at the end of the Gospel of Mathew "I am with you always, to the close of the age" is not an absolute promise of assistance for the indiscriminate use of power to convert others and baptize them; rather it is a checking presence and caution given to the disciples and to the Church at large as well as to her missionaries not to go about conquering the world. The Church has to be a sign and sacrament of God's presence in the world, the God whom Jesus presented with a passion and a persuasion as the Father and Mother of the whole humankind and of the entire cosmos in the ongoing process of history.

Being a religious minority in India is not so much a miserable experience nor is it something to be regretted. In fact, to be a minority in a land of religious pluralism is in itself something to be appreciated and this fact should lead the minority community to a dignified living. Unity in diversity and the ability to respond to a sense of realism are very important for a minority to keep pace with the growth process of a nation. All religions have to work together to respect universal values of justice, equality, non-violence, love and compassion. In this minority religions can play a significant role. The followers of all religions have to be aware that they are co-pilgrims guiding each other towards the one transcendent goal of life which is common to all religions. It is in this common pilgrimage that the Christians should share their spiritual experience with others and collaborate with them in the building up of the nation, thereby fully committed to national integration. In fact, Christianity had failed very much on this issue of national integration because of its colonial face during several centuries. They have to become fully aware of their solidarity with the rest of the nation. Only through this national integration could Christianity become an integral part of the religious patrimony of this country.[13]

Christianity has to its credit a message of universalism as its basic gospel of *lokasamgraha*. Jesus preached this gospel based on the Father/Motherhood of God and the universal brother/sisterhood of the whole humankind transcending the barriers of caste, colour and creed. In this sense, Christianity is more than a religion; it is a way of life and a movement which transcends all religions and is at home with every religion. The primary preoccupation of this movement is not so much about it being a minority and its privileges, but rather about its commitment to the cause of the humanity and to the nation where it exists and operates. Its existence in India demands, first of all, that it dedicates itself to the cause of the nation. At the same time, this commitment to the nation should not be understood primarily as a narrow nationalism. Rather it should be a nationalism that is built on the values of universalism and integral humanism. It should be a nationalism that respects, acknowledges and fosters the identities of India's diverse peoples, cultures and religions. Christianity should build up the courage to take up these universal concerns of the Indian reality, characterized by a variety of marginalized and oppressed minorities and subaltern groups. In fact, the God of the Bible and the

---

[13] The author acknowledges his profound indebtedness to many relevant and useful ideas in the "The Challenge of Hindutva : An Indian Christian Response" which is the concluding Statement of the Indian Theological Association during its 23rd Annual Meeting held in Dharmaram Vidya Kshetram, April 26-30, 2000.

central biblical message invite Christians to defend the identities of the oppressed and the marginalized.

Being a religious minority is equally conducive to taking up the cause of effectively promoting the cause of human rights by joining hands with all peoples, movements and associations working for the defense of human and civil rights. Genuine Christian faith demands that they collaborate with the poor and the marginalized in the struggle for liberation and empowerment. Following in the footsteps of Jesus of Nazareth, Christians should live and work in solidarity with subaltern groups. This alone would enable the Church to be in reality a Church of the poor and the marginalized and an authentic Indian Church. Closely associated with the cause of the marginalized, is the place of the women in the Indian society. With its great ideology of the equality of men and women (Gal 3:28), Christians must take up the cause of the women, which many religions in India are not very much interested in. In order to realize this, the Church must, first of all, remove all that is discriminatory in its own system regarding women and promote a sense of dignity of women in the larger society and its operation.

The Church as the "Little Flock" (Lk 12:32)

What the Indian Christians now are urgently in need of is an encouraging theology and a consequent sense of the "little flock" and all that it implies. Jesus told his disciples: "Do not be afraid, little flock, for it is your Father's good pleasure to give you the kingdom. Sell your possessions, and give alms. Make purses for yourselves that do not wear out, an unfailing treasure in heaven, where no thief comes near and no moth destroys" (Lk 12:32-33). When Jesus pronounced these words of wisdom and encouragement to his disciples more than two thousand years ago, the community of the followers of Jesus was a little flock and even after two millennia the Christians constitute only a minority in the family of religions, and it shall always remain as a little flock. What is imperative for this little flock is not so much the preoccupation with its minority status and its disadvantages, but rather its mission and task in the wider humanity. The Church is the community of Jesus' disciples who are called together by his word and animated by his Spirit to continue his mission and carry it among the various nations of the world. The task of the Church is to create a new human community, which is characterized by love, freedom, equality, justice and peace. Any preoccupation on the part of the Church with numerical expansion runs counter to its sacred mission of bearing witness to God's reign, which transcends the boundaries of any religion. The Church is providentially destined to remain in India and in the world as a "little flock", and the fulfillment of its mission does not lie in the strength of its members but in the power God's love and truth operating through it and transforming the humankind.

This means that the Church must make all efforts to remove every trace of triumphalism, exclusivism, and a certain attitude of superiority in its teachings, evangelizing activities and styles of the functioning of its institutions. Christianity should be basically a dialogical community. Consequently, it has to avoid any tendency to become a monolithic and mono-cultural group of people; rather it has to foster all kinds of dialogue with other religions and movements. This dialogical mission also means that Christians have to become agents of reconciliation and harmony among the various groups. They have to join hands with the majority of the citizens of this country who are basically peace loving and co-operating. They have to avoid all forms of proselytization which is a very questionable exercise in the context of a widespread religious pluralism. Vatican II has made it very clear in its *Declaration on Religious Freedom:* "In spreading religious faith and introducing religious practices, everyone ought at all times to refrain from any manner of action which could seem to carry a hint of coercion or a kind of persuasion that would be dishonourable or unworthy, especially when dealing with poor and uneducated people. Such a manner of actions would have to be considered an abuse of one's right and a violation of the rights of others".[14] The various Churches and Christian denominations have had invited enough of criticism regarding their evangelizing and missionary activities during the past several centuries, especially after the arrival of the Portuguese and the British people in this country and it is now an opportune time for all Christians to cultivate a new culture of national integration. Thereby the Christians in this country will be happier to experience that their status as a religious minority is not at all a disgrace and a burden; but rather a blessing and a call to be more tolerant and co-operating with all men and women of good will.

---

[14] *Declaration on Religious Freedom*, no. 4.

V

BIBLICAL INTERPRETATION: CHANCE AND CHALLENGE IN OUR TIMES

The Acts of the Apostles narrates the story of Philip, one of the seven appointed servants of the table, how he had to enter into a discussion with an Ethiopian official about the interpretation of a biblical passage he was reading from the book of Isaiah. To the question Philip raised to the Ethiopian: "Do you understand what you are reading?" his answer was "How can I unless someone guides me?" (Acts 8:31-32). Then he invited Philip to sit near him and explain the passage to him, the result of which was that the Ethiopian understood the fuller meaning of what he was reading as related to the person of Jesus of Nazareth. The he insisted on his becoming a believer in Jesus Christ. In another story in Matthew we read about the disciples of Jesus requesting him: "Explain to us the parable of the weeds" (Matt 13:36). Luke narrates the story of two disciples of Jesus going away from Jerusalem after they had been disillusioned about their expectations about Jesus of Nazareth. On the way they were encountered by the risen Jesus and they gradually came to understand that Jesus was risen from the dead and so they went back to the community at Jerusalem. These stories taken from the Bible itself show that the interpretation of the Bible was an ongoing exercise of the Christian community from the very beginning of the New Testament times. The same tradition of interpreting the Bible continued in the early Church as well as during the Patristic times and it is considered as one of the most important exercises of the teaching office of the Church and her theologians in our times.

Since the Bible is the Word of God in human language, there is the need of it being interpreted to the readers to enable them to understand the inner message of this divine and human reality. Whereas during the earlier centuries the interpretation of the Bible was relatively a simpler exercise for the reason that the Bible was understood exclusively as the Word of God, in our times it has become a very demanding and complex scientific exercise. Vatican II through its Dogmatic Constitution *Dei Verbum* has given a new impetus to the scientific study and interpretation of the Bible. It states: Those who search out the intention of the sacred writers must, among other things, have regard for literary forms. For truth is proposed and expressed in a variety of ways, whether its form is that of prophecy, poetry, or some other type of speech. The interpreter must investigate what meaning the sacred writer intended to express and actually expressed in particular circumstances as he used contemporary literary forms in accordance with the situation of his own time and culture. For the correct understanding of what the sacred author wanted to assert, due attention must be paid to the customary and characteristic styles of perceiving, speaking, and narrating which prevailed at the time of the sacred writer, and to the customs men normally followed at that period in their everyday dealings with one another".[1]

Paul wrote to the Corinthians: "Now is the acceptable time; now is the day of salvation" (2 Cor 6:2). It seems that this statement of Paul about the *now* as something important is specifically true of the new climate about the interpretation of the Bible in the Church taken as a whole. This is particularly true of the Roman Catholic Church in our times after centuries of its relegating the Bible to some cautious areas, precisely because of a defensive and reactionary attitude to the Protestant doctrine of *sola Scriptura* as well as their its bold attempts towards a scientific interpretation of the Bible during the past several centuries. But now the situation has entirely changed and scientific study and interpretation of the Bible is an area in which ecumenism has been very fruitfully established with the result that there is no more question of Roman Catholic interpretation of the Bible as opposed to or as different from the Protestant interpretation. What all try to exercise is a scientific and pastoral interpretation of biblical books and in this area a lot of cooperation and team work is being planned and executed.

A Brief Historical Survey

As it happens with regard to many doctrinal developments, both theological and secular, the present encouraging tone of the teaching office of the Roman Catholic Church regarding the scientific study and interpretation of the Bible is the end product of more than half a century of hesitation, anxiety and fear about the biblical studies. For the Roman

---

[1] Cf. *Dei Verbum* art. 12.

Catholic Church it took more time to understand the fact that Bible is the Word of God in human language and that the interpreter must pay attention to both these dimensions of the text of the Bible. As a result of some courageous endeavours initiated by the Pontifical Biblical Commission after the publication of the Encyclical *Divino Afflante Spiritu* in 1943, exegetes and theologians in the Roman Catholic Church are enjoying greater academic freedom regarding the scientific study of the Bible, the Old and New Testaments.

The first official teaching of the Church in recent times regarding the study of the Bible published toward the end of the 19th century CE is *Providentissimus Deus* by Leo XIII in 1893. In this document the Pope recognized the services rendered by the scientific methods of biblical research and expressed his desire that these methods are used for a deeper understanding of the sacred books. But he maintained that the Bible is the Word of God and is therefore infallible, and so scientific research can never ignore this fact. Hence he said that no interpretation can neglect the criteria of faith and tradition. On the whole, this encyclical was based on the firm conviction that there can be no contradiction between the Word of God and the findings of sciences, provided on both sides the experts honestly seek the truth and are aware of their own limitations. God who created nature and is the author of the Bible cannot contradict himself. It should be said that the encyclical was on the whole negative towards the critical and scientific study of the Bible. In 1902 Pope Leo XIII established the Pontifical Biblical Commission for promoting the study of the Bible and at the same time to keep a vigil over the Roman Catholic study of the Bible.[2] Consequent to the constituting of this Commission a series of enquiries about the various aspects of the study of the Bible were sent to this Commission seeking answers, and most of the questions which had some reference to a scientific study of the Bible, were answered with a simple *"negative"*.[3]

---

[2] The very name of the Apostolic Letter *Vigilantiae* through which the Pontifical Biblical Commission was established shows that the ultimate purpose of the Commission was vigilance rather than encouragement.

[3] Cf. Dennis J. Murphy (Ed), *The Church and the Bible* (Bangalore: Theological Publications in India, 2001) pp.94-162. It is interesting to note that in 1955 there came out directives which indirectly agreed to rescind the binding character of the responses which the Pontifical Biblical Commission gave to questions which were typical of the conservative atmosphere. Cf. Dennis J. Murphy, *op.cit. pp. 296-297.*

The beginning of the 20th century CE witnessed a more serious situation in the Roman Catholic Church with the emergence of a theological and spiritual movement known as 'modernism' which, among other things, subscribed to a liberal attitude toward biblical criticism and exegesis. The encyclical *Pascendi* by Pius X in 1907 and the decree *Lamentabili* of the Holy Office in 1907 condemned several positions held by the followers of this movement. In 1909 Pope Pius X through his Apostolic Letter *Vinea Electa* established the Pontifical Biblical Institute with elaborate rules and regulations about biblical studies. On the whole, the result of these developments was only more control over the study of the Bible than encouragement. In 1920 Pope Benedit XV, to mark the fifteen-hundredth anniversary of the death of Jerome, the great biblical scholar as well as the translator and the interpreter of the Bible, published the encyclical *Spiritus Paraclitus* in 1920. The biblical doctrine developed here is essentially that of the encyclical of Leo XIII. Perhaps it went a step backward in its attempt to establish that inspiration extends to both religious as well as profane matters. The period that followed this document was a dark one in the history of Catholic biblical scholarship. It was clear that the public was also involved in controlling the scientific study of the Bible. The title of an anonymous brochure sent in 1941 to the College of the Cardinals and Superior Generals of the Religious Orders read: "A most serious danger for the Church and for souls. The critical-scientific method in the study and interpretation of Holy Scripture, its fatal deviations and aberrations".

It was during these hard times that Pope Pius XII took a strong decision in favour of the scientific study of the Bible, and in 1943, to mark the 50th anniversary of the encyclical *Providentissimus Deus* published the encyclical *Divino Afflante Spiritu,* which is still considered as a land mark in the history of biblical interpretation and also the magna carta of modern Catholic biblical studies. In this document the knowledge and mastery of biblical and oriental languages are recommended; the position of the Catholic Church with regard to the Latin Vulgate is clarified. Catholic exegetes are encouraged to make proper use of textual criticism and the literary analysis of the Bible according to literary genres and form criticism. In fact, the teaching of the Dogmatic Constitution on Divine Revelation regarding the scientific study of the Bible, which we have referred to above, is a resuming and a confirmation of the bold steps taken by Pius XII through this encyclical almost 22 years back. Seven years after the publication of the encyclical in 1950 the same Pope promulgated the encyclical *Humani Generis* giving some more specific orientation about the scientific study of the Bible. This encyclical is closely related to a letter written by the Secretary of the Pontifical Biblical Commission to Cardinal Suhard, Archbishop of Paris, in 1948 about the sources of the Pentateuch and the historicity of the first eleven chapters of Genesis. Though the general tone of this encyclical is one of caution, a careful study of this important document shows that a great deal of freedom is given to exegetes to carry on their scientific study of the Bible. The Pope also conceded the possibility of the evolution of the human body from lower forms of life, provided it is recognized that the human life principle is the result of the immediate act of God. The question regarding polygenism was left rather open, although the document seems to be favouring monogenism on theological grounds.[4] Instructions concerning prudence in the interpretation of the Bible continued to be published from Rome, such as Instruction concerning biblical associations and conventions by the Pontifical Biblical Commission in 1955, the address of Pope John XXIII to the staff and students of the Pontifical Biblical Institute on the occasion of golden Jubilee in 1960. The Pope reminded the Institute about the need of rigorous scholarship with complete submission to the deposit of faith and teachings of the Magisterium of the Church.

Very soon a new wave of negativism and reaction to the scientific study of the Bible developed in the Roman circles, and it began to threaten the little progress that was made in some circles in Catholic biblical scholarship with the encouragement given by Pope Pius XII. The first of this shock was a *Monitum* issued by the Holy Office in 1961, now known as the Congregation for the Doctrine of the Faith, cautioning and warning Catholic biblical scholars that they should not call into question the narratives of the Gospels regarding the sayings and deeds of Christ Jesus. This *Monitum* was a sequel to the heated controversy between the progressive Jesuit-run Pontifical Biblical Institute and the conservative Lateran university in Rome, a controversy occasioned by an article of Father Alonso Schökel in an Italian journal. The *Monitum* in no way wanted to discourage Roman Catholic exegetes from using modern critical techniques developed by the biblical scholars in other Churches. However, it was felt in many circles that Catholic exegesis was going to

---

[4] The difficulty of accepting polygenism lies in the fact that it is not easy to combine the traditional doctrine of original sin with the theory of polygenism.

suffer a setback, and the fear was all the more growing when Vatican II started in 1962 with its problematic schema on the "Sources of Revelation".

When the flames of the controversy had subsided and the atmosphere had been once again cleared, the Pontifical Biblical Commission issued an elaborate 'Instruction on the Historical Truth of Gospels on 14th May 1964, which once again became a major breakthrough in the study of the New Testament, especially for the interpretation of the Gospels.[5] This document clearly speaks about three important stages in the long process of the formation of the Gospels, namely, the stage in which Jesus lived, spoke and worked in Palestine; the stage in which the early Church preserved this living tradition about Jesus in its preaching, teaching, worship and missionary endeavours; and finally, the stage in which the evangelists using their own theological genius and literary talents composed the four Gospels as we have them today. In fact, this document was a refined form of approving the scientific contributions of two eminent Protestant scholars, Rudolf Bultmann and Martin Dibelius who around 1918, had proposed their radical theories about the formation of the Synoptic Gospels. The less official nature of this document of the Pontifical Biblical Commission once again received a clear and official approval in 1965 by Vatican II in its Dogmatic Constitution on Divine Revelation when it speaks about the complex process through which the Gospels came to be written. About the final stage of writing the Gospels by the evangelists the document states: "The sacred authors wrote the four Gospels, selecting some things from the many which had been handed on by word of mouth or in writing, reducing some of them to a synthesis, explicating some things in view of the situation of their Churches, and preserving th form of proclamation but always in such fashion that they told us the honest truth about Jesus".[6]

In 1974 Pope Paul VI reconstituted the Pontifical Biblical Commission as a really international body of biblical scholars and in his first exhortation to them the Pope spoke about the duty of Catholic exegetes to present to the people of God the message of revelation, to set

---

[5] More about this Roman Document cf. Joseph Pathrapankal, *Understanding the Gospels Today* (Bangalore: Dharmaram Publications, 1977).

[6] *Dei Verbum* art. 19.

forth the meaning of the Word of God in itself and in its relation to the humans today, to give access to the Word, beyond the envelopes of semantic sings and cultural syntheses, sometimes far removed from the culture and problems of our times. It was an invitation to the exegetes to combine the diachronic and synchronic dimensions of biblical interpretation, to see the meaning of the Word of God not only in its original setting but also in its relation to the issues and problems of our times.[7] It means that the Bible is to be interpreted taking into account not only the context of the author but also the context and needs of the readers because the Word of God is meant for the people for whom it was written and who try to derive strength and support for their life from the Bible.[8]

A major outcome of this growing concern about the scientific study and interpretation of the Bible and its pastoral application was the presentation of a document by the Pontifical Biblical Commission in April 1993 to Pope John Paul II, known as the *Interpretation of the Bible in the Church* and its later publication in November 1993. It gives a detailed survey of methods and approaches to the study of the Bible in the Catholic Church which is followed by some hermeneutical questions as well as the presentation of some specific criteria for the interpretation of the Bible in the Catholic Church as well as an invitation to a meaningful interpretation of the Bible in the life of the Church. The publication of this mature document must guide the ongoing work of the Catholic exegetes. In a certain sense it can be said that it is the climaxing stage of a painful and fruitful process of approaching the study of the Bible in the Catholic Church. It is the long story of one century, the first half of which was nebulous and negative and the second half of it was encouraging and positive. The new focus of biblical interpretation is on alternative methods and approaches and gradual abandoning of the exclusive use of the historical-critical method. The document tries to indicate the paths mosot appropriate for arriving at an interpretation of the Bible as faithful and possible to its character both divine and human and also to examine all the methods which are likely to contribute

---

[7] Cf. *Voice of the Church*, Changanacherry, May 1974, pp. 681-682.

[8] Cf. "Interpretation of the Word: God's Word, the human word and the interpreter's word" in *Text and Context in Biblical Interpreation* (Bangalore: Dharmaram Publications, 1993) pp. 1-16.

effectively to the task of making available the riches contained in the biblical texts.

New Challenges and Chances

When we look through the long and complex history of the interpretation of the Bible in the Church, we can also see three major stages in the understanding of the Bible. This is true of all Churches. But the time factor in the various Churches is different. The first stage is when the Bible was understood exclusively as the word of God; the second stage is when the Bible is understood as the word of God in human words, where the human word dimension was thoroughly studied under a series of 'criticisms', such as historical criticism, literary criticism, form criticism, redaction criticism and textual criticism. A third stage is now gradually emerging and this is what we may call the time when the Bible as the divine word and the human author word is to be understood and applied in the context of the reader and the interpreter. This stage also has to be scientific and there is no question of confusing fanciful ideas with scientific data. Here it is question of discovering the meaning and message of the Bible for the living context of the men and women of our times.

Together with these developments there has been also a major shift of emphasis in the understanding of that divine phenomenon of inspiration, which is responsible for making the Bible entirely different from other world literature. Basing the concept of inspiration on the Greek word *theopneustos* (2 Tim 3:16), it was maintained in the past that the writers of the various books of the Bible, while they were engaged in their writing, were given a special divine assistance of formulating what they wrote as the word of God. The immediate effect of this divine assistance was understood as 'inerrancy' of the Bible, namely, the absence of errors of all kinds. Hence the effort of all exegetes was to establish the truth of the Bible against those who were attributing errors of various kinds, such as historical and scientific errors. Here it is to be remembered that inspiration is not something that is limited to the writing down of the books of the Bible. The entire process of the formation of the Bible, both the Old and the New Testaments, was a divinely inspired one, the stage of the oral traditions, the process of the formation of the written traditions, the various literary editions behind the final writing of the books of the Bible. The most important effect of this divine guidance is that the Bible is the Word of God, that it gives us a divine message that leads its readers on the path of salvation. Hence the truth of the Bible is not any truth, it is the salvific truth. It means that the there can be historical errors and scientific errors in the various narratives of the Bible. But there is dimension of truth that transcends all these limitations and it is through the eyes of faith that the children of the Church have to arrive at this truth.

Now that biblical scholarship has reached a stage of maturity and self-identity, new challenges are to be faced. There is a growing awareness among biblical exegetes that there is need of a more relevant and meaningful hermeneutics to cope up with the social, cultural and religious aspirations of humans in our times. Right from the time of the Fathers of the Church, several theories of interpretation have been applied to the understanding of the Bible. Ever since the scientific revolution of the 16th and 17th centuries, which ushered in the modern era, it was historical criticism that has been the dominant method of biblical exegesis. Side by side with this scientific method there has been also what is known as the fundamentalist approach to the interpretation of the Bible whereby a too literal sense of the Bible was defended; and it was seen as a safeguard against the liberal interpretation of the Bible. Both these approaches subscribe to an objectivist, one dimensional hermeneutics, which assumes that the text of the Bible has only one true meaning, wholly independent of the cultural conditioning of the reader and the interpreter. The fundamentalist, for whom the Bible is God's inspired Word spoken directly to and recorded immediately by the biblical author, would find true meaning in the various literal sense of a biblical text as this is read by believing readers within the tradition of their community. The scientific critic, on the other hand, keenly aware that the Bible is the end product of a long and complex process of oral tradition and literary editing, would look for this true meaning of a biblical text in its original author-setting, namely, in the meaning which was intended by the original author, and has now to be recovered from the layers of interpretation that have been accumulated around it, by a diligent application of the historical critical method.

Whereas biblical fundamentalism is being more and more discarded and discredited, because of its naivety and lack of scientific basis, although it has its own adherents both in Catholic and Protestant circles, especially as a reaction to liberal thinking, historical critical method has been exercising tremendous influence on biblical exegesis for the past few hundred years as the standard method. But of late, this critical method is also beginning to lose its dominant hold on biblical exegesis. There is a growing awareness among biblical scholars that the method, though still useful, is not really adequate for interpreting a text which is not purely scientific, but basically religious. Historical criticism uses historical methods to interpret a religious text, and there is an anomaly in it. A method meant for obtaining exact scientific information is being used to interpret a text which aims at the personal transformation of the readers through the response of their faith. As a matter of fact, a biblical text is meant to be interpreted by successive generations of readers in their respective social, cultural and religious situations for the ongoing response to their contemporary and living situations. The biblical text therefore has not only a past history, accessible to historical criticism but also an openness to the present and to the future, which far surpasses the realities and the demands of the past. The historical critical method does not sufficiently take into account this dynamic and open character of the biblical text.

The same is true of some other methods of biblical interpretation current during the past decades, such as biblical structuralism and rhetorical criticism. While recognizing the services rendered by these and similar methods, it must be forcefully established that all these methods have not succeeded in making the biblical text communicate the message it is supposed to give to men and women in our times. Whenever criticism abandons the emancipating and liberating meaning with which it once began, it becomes an orthodoxy and system in its own right, committed to the momentum of its own technical apparatus, and indifferent to the life questions which gave birth to these texts themselves. In fact, in the past, for many, biblical scholarship had become more a luxury good, largely unrelated to the struggles of the real people of our times, fighting for liberation and a dignified human living. Scholars, as a rule, look only to the Universities and to other centers of academic pursuit as well as to their peers in the professional societies and organizations as their community of accountability. The ever-increasing technical complexity of biblical studies, with its formidable apparatus of textual and historical criticism, comparative grammar and philology, reconstruction of the historical background through geography, archeology, papyrology, its recourse to source criticism, form criticism, tradition criticism and redaction criticism all tend to display a sense of complacency that there are not problems beyond these hermeneutical problems, that all is well when there is no exegetical problem. This was true of the majority of biblical scholars all over the world, especially in the affluent countries of the West. There were a few exceptions, and they were clearly exceptions. It is precisely here that we come to the problem of the text in relation to the context, the context of the reader and the interpreter. Enough has been said and done about the context of the human author of the Bible. Whereas biblical fundamentalism pays no attention to the context in which the biblical texts were written, historical critical method was exclusively concerned with the analysis of the text within the context of its origin. Structuralism, on the other hand, totally abandoned the context in favour of the deep structures which constitute the text as it stands no, while rhetorical criticism tries to study the Bible as literature, exposing it to the methods used by literary critics in their study of creative literary works.

The Dynamics of the Context

The context of the text, as it is going to be explained here, is to be clearly distinguished from what is generally known as the *Sitz im Leben* of the biblical text. In fact, what is proposed here is something entirely different from the original context. The context here means the context of the reader and the interpreter. Hence contextualization here means the transcending of the original context by which the text is made to speak to the context of the reader and the interpreter. Here it is question of a situative context. The biblical text, as the inspired word of God, is meant to be further interpreted by successive generations of readers in their respective social, cultural and religious situations. The biblical text therefore has not only a past history accessible to historical criticism, but also an openness to the present and to the future, which far surpasses the past and its concerns. As we have already seen, the objectivism of the historical method prevents it from appreciating the role, the reader and the interpreter have in constituting the total meaning of a text, and so it remains blind to the authentically new meaning that a text may have to acquire as its is read in ever new situations. The text has a life of its own as it moves through history, assuming new dimensions and connotations as it relates itself to new horizons and contexts.

We may explain this approach to the situative contextualization as a process and exercise of de-contextualization of the original diachronic context in favour of a re-contextualization to the new synchronic context, through which the biblical text continues to speak to our times without at the same time losing its original meaning, message and challenge. What is aimed at here is not a demythologization of the word from the event, as Bultmann has proposed, but rather the re-application of the original message to the new situation with its new challenges, problems and promises. The meaning of the text was not exhausted by what was intended by the author or what the text, in fact, says; whether the author explicitly intended it or not. It is also what the readers today understand as part of the dynamic meaning of the text within their own historical, cultural and religious context. This is particularly true of the Bible which is the word of God entrusted to the Church as the source of her life and vitality, and this inspired word of God has within itself a dynamism to take on new meanings and open us new horizons of ideas through its encounter with new contexts and situations in the process of history.

A very important consideration of this synchronic contextualization in biblical exegesis is what may be called an 'ecclesial hermeneutics', namely, a hermeneutics which is guided and inspired by the reality of the living Church. The source from which the Church derives the vitality and energy for this ministry of the word is the Holy Spirit, the same Spirit of God who guided the entire process of the recording of the various books of the Bible. The formation of the various books of the Old and New Testaments was a social event of the faith communities of Israel and the early Church, an event in which the whole community was involved and inspired by God. The writers of the various books of the Bible acted as representatives of these faith communities, and their concern it was to articulate the faith of the community they were representing, at the same time making use of their own thinking patterns and literary skills. The same community dimension of the people of God as well as the representative role of the exegetes and theologians have to be recognized in the interpretation of the Bible in our times.

Paradigms of Contextualization

We have a clear example of this synchronic and situative contextualization of the writing of the gospel in the theology of Luke. What Luke did was to transfer the Palestinian context of the ministry of Jesus to the context and concerns of the wider Roman Empire. Hence the birth of Jesus and the ministry of John the Baptist are placed in the larger context of the Roman Empire. Later on, the specific socio-economic issues of the immediate context of the ministry of Jesus in Palestine are seen in relation to the corresponding issues of the wider Roman Empire, and the social stance of Jesus in Palestine to the various issues of his society is presented as having a corresponding influence also on similar and related issues in the larger context of the Roman Empire. What Luke did was to show that the ministry of Jesus in Palestine has a relevance and bearing not only for the narrow confines of Palestine but also for the entire Roman Empire, which was the *oikoumene* of the then-known world. For Luke, Jesus was the saviour of both the Jews and the Greeks. Hence Luke is particularly concerned about seeing Jesus as transcending his own Jewish identity through his tolerant and appreciative attitude towards the Samaritans and Gentiles. This, besides a mission of the Twelve, common to all Synoptists (Lk 9:1-6), Luke presents the Lord as sending our 70 disciples "into every town and village where he himself was about to come" (Lk 10:1), through which Luke was looking forward to the universal influence of the gospel preached by Jesus. This effort to contextualize the gospel to the wide Roman Empire also enabled Luke to present the early Church as a dynamic community committed to an uncompromising testimony to Christ in the latter half of the first century of the Common Era until it reached its climactic affirmation through the ministry of Paul.

Taking inspiration from this exercise of early Christian contextualization, exegetes today have to develop a new sense of relating the text of the Bible to the context of their ministry. We have had enough of historical criticism and other critical methods, and the valid insights of these methods have to be maintained and applied to the study and interpretation of the Bible by all serious exegetes and biblical scholars. But beyond that exegetes and theologians have to face a larger missionary reality of the world which they have to transform by the power of the word of God. A synchronic and contextualized interpretation of the Bible will very much help the Christians all over the world to develop a more positive attitude to life and its problems and challenges, precisely because thereby they can approach the Bible in the context of the life-setting of the reader and the interpreter. Since Christians are trained to look to the word of God in the Bible for deriving vitality and orientation for their life and also for solving the problems encountered in their life, it is very important that they are also trained to have a broader and contextualized understanding of it in relation to their living context. Moreover, such an approach will open up new horizons of insights which will make the mission of the Church in the world more relevant and meaningful.

Although the scientific aspect of the approach to the Bible explained here is not as evident as in the case of historical critical method and other recognized scientific methods, the pastoral relevance of this approach as well as the liberating value of this method of analysis cannot be called into question because it is within the concrete context of the mission of the Church that we have to approach the Bible. It is to be kept in mind that in the Bible we are primarily dealing with a religious text which stands above the criteria and characteristics of any human literature. The presence of the Church in the world becomes meaningful and relevant only when the Church, her theologians and exegetes succeed in reading the signs of the times and thereby make the Bible and theological issues intelligible within the context of our times. We have to allow the word of God to accomplish its liberating and transforming power (Is 55:10-11), realizing that the word of God is living and active, sharper than any two-edged sword, piercing until it can enter into the subtle distinction between soul and spirit in a human person and penetrate into the joints and marrow of the human body (Heb 4:12). Realized as God's powerful word in the past, the Bible releases its saving and transforming power in the present by the response it makes to the living contexts of our time and its challenges.

A typical case of this contextualized application of the Bible to the contemporary world we have in the manner in which Gustavo Gutierrez looked at the Bible when he had to face the challenge of interpreting the situation of his country in the light of religion and its Scriptures which were supposed to define that religion for him and for his people. Confronted as he was with the challenge of his society and complex history of his country, he reacted to the established principles of interpreting religion and its relation to his society, principles which were considered sacrosanct and were handed down through centuries without any reference to time, culture and the needs of the society. His was a reaction to theology understood as wisdom and rational knowledge as well as the rejection of the Bible understood as a source of piety and abstract spirituality. What he did was to establish theology as a critical reflection on historical praxis based on the principles of the gospel and experiences of men and women committed to a process of liberation in the oppressed and exploited land of Latin America. The power he released through his bold and radical interpretation of the gospel with a reference to the context of the life of his people is making inroads in many countries of the so-called Third World and is challenging men and women to commit themselves to a more radical and relevant interpretation of their religion and its Scriptures.

A recent work of John P. Meier about Jesus as a marginal Jew[9] has raised several questions about the religious identity of Jesus of Nazareth and his relation to Judaism as a whole. Since he was born and brought up in the territory of Galilee, which was technically known as the Galilee of the Gentiles (Mt 4:15), Jesus could not and did not belong to the category of those, for whom the Law of Moses was the ultimate norm and controlling factor of religious identity. The Jews in this area were surrounded by a fair number of Greeks and Gentiles and also good amount of Hellenistic culture and world vision. Consequently, these Jews would adhere only to the basics of their religion and religious practices. More than that, they were also prepared to see and appreciate goodness and virtue not only among their fellow humans, but also among the followers of other religious traditions. So it is quite natural that Jesus also could appreciate goodness and a meaningful faith in the centurion who went to Jesus seeking from him a healing for his servant who was lying paralyzed at home (Mt 8:5-13). Hence Jesus was also spontaneous in offering his service to him. The same can be said about Jesus' attitude towards the Samaritans who were, in general, disliked by the Jews. Hence in his discussion with the Samaritan woman Jesus spells out his profound convictions about what religion and worship ultimately mean (John 4:21-24). What Jesus told the Samaritan woman could be understood as an epitome of religion and worship not only for the Jews and the Samaritans but also for the followers of all religions, then as well as now. This could be summarized as follows: In the past, the followers

---

[9] John P. Meier, *A Marginal Jew* (New York: Doubleday, Vol I, 1991; Vol II, 1994). Other similar works are: Geza Vermes, *Jesus and the World of Judaism* (London: SCM Press, 1983) and *Jesus the Jew* (London: SCM Press, 1973); James H. Charelsworth, *Jesus' Jewishness* (Ed) (New York: The Crossword Publishing Company, 1991).

of various religious groups had their own ways of worshipping God, often in a context of rivalry and competition. But from now on, religion itself and worship, in particular, have to assume a new meaning and a new expression. Worship is no more to be localized and monopolized by a few people who think that they are the privileged and authorized ones, from whom all others have to learn and practise the essentials of worship. Rather, worship must be the exercise of the freedom of the spirit for all humans whoever and wherever they are. All what happened in the past in the history of Judaism and Samaritans were expressions of rivalry and competition, either one claiming superiority over the other, or one condemning the other as false and illegitimate. The time has now come for all to rise up from such religious enslavement and inaugurate a new era of worship with the power of the genuine operation of the spirit of God, which is encompassing the universe of faiths and religious traditions.

A Re-reading of John 12:20-27

It is against the background of the above considerations about religion and worship that we now try to analyse John 12:20-27, which is a very significant story that throws much light on the outgoing and centrifugal attitude of Jesus of Nazareth towards the followers of other religions. But before we begin this contextualized analysis of the story it is very important to establish an important synchronic principle of biblical interpretation that is being discussed, mainly in the religiously and culturally pluralistic situations of our times. It is related to the new demands of contextualization and actualization that are being applied in biblical interpretation. It should be kept in mind that contextualization here means something more than what this concept originally meant in biblical studies. Here it means the transcending of the original context and the *Sitz im Leben* of the biblical text, through which text is made to speak anew to the new context of the reader and the interpreter. Here it is a question of what may be called a situative context of the reader and the interpreter. It means that the biblical text is to be further interpreted by successive generations of readers in their own respective social, cultural and religions situations without losing sight of the original context and its original meaning.[10] It means that the text has not only a past history

---

[10] Cf. Joseph Pathrapankal, "Interpretation of the Word: God's Word, the Human Word and the Interpreter's Word" in *Text and Context in Biblical Interpretation* (Bangalore: Dharmaram Publications, 1993) pp. 1-16.

accessible to us through textual and historical criticism, but also an openness to the present and to the future which far surpasses the issues of the past. In fact, very often the objectivism of the historical critical method prevents it from appreciating the role the reader and the interpreter have in establishing the total meaning of the text and it remains blind to the authentically new meaning and challenge that a text may have to acquire as it is read in ever new situations.[11] The text has a life of its own as it moves through history, assuming new dimensions and connotations as it relates itself to new situations and socio-religious as well as cultural contexts. We may explain this approach to situative contextualization as a process of discovering the new synchronic context by which a text continues to speak to our times without at the same time losing the original meaning, message and challenge. In fact, the meaning of a text is not exhausted by what was intended by the author or what the text in fact says. It is also what the readers today understand as part of the dynamic meaning of the text within their own historical, cultural, social and religious context. This is particularly true of the Bible which is the Word of God entrusted to the Church as the source of her life and vitality. This Word of God has within itself a dynamism to take on new meanings and new horizons of ideas through its encounter with new contexts in a pluralistic world.[12]

The story we analyse here is about some Greeks who had gone to Jerusalem for worshipping in the Temple and had listened to the teaching of Jesus in the Temple area. They were religiously well-disposed persons who could appreciate the religious practices of Judaism and had come to Jerusalem to take part in the festival of the Dedication. As was the case with the temple police who confessed to the Jewish authorities about the unique teaching of Jesus: "Never has anyone spoken like this" (John 7:46), so also these Greeks were fascinated by the authentic and challenging teaching of Jesus. Hence it was only natural

---

[11] Cf. G. Meier, *The End of the Historical Critical Method* (St. Louis: Concordia, 1977); P. Stuhlmacher, *Historical Criticism and Theological Interpretation of Scripture* (Philadelphia: Fortress Press, 1977); E. Krentz, *The Historical Critical Method* (Philadelphia: Fortress Press, 1975).

[12] "Hermeneutics is the task of always coming back to the text under new circumstances and in new situations and it is always a re-reading of scriptures and of ourselves, our world, our society and our history" (Joseph Pathrapankal, Editorial, *Journal of Dharma* 5 (1980) p.2.

that they wanted to meet Jesus. It is also important to remember that this story is narrated towards the end of the Book of Signs (John 1-12) where John concludes a series of signs performed by Jesus, through which he invited the crowd to believe in him and his message. As a concluding event of this major section of the Gospel, it seems that this story has its own theological and pedagogical purpose. In fact, it is in this story that Jesus emerges in his most sublime and transcendent dimensions of religious identity, as we shall try to explain below:

> *Now among those who went up to worship at the festival were some Greeks. They came to Philip, who was from Bethsaida in Galilee, and said to him, 'Sir, we wish to see Jesus'. Philip went and told Andrew; then Andrew and Philip went and told Jesus. Jesus answered them, 'The hour has come for the Son of Man to be glorified. Very truly, I tell you, unless a grain of wheat falls into the earth and dies, it remains just a single grain; but if it dies, it bears much fruit. Those who love their life lose it, and those who hate their life in this world will keep it for eternal life. Whoever serves me must follow me, and where I am, there will my servant be also. Whoever serves me, the Father will honour. 'Now my soul is troubled. And what should I say – 'Father, save me from this hour? No, it is for this reason that I have come to this hour" (John 12:20-27)*

Raymond E. Brown, in his elaborate commentary on John,[13] has referred to the theological meaning of this scene. According to him, the *coming* (italics in the original) of the Gentiles is so theologically important that the writer never tells us if they got to see Jesus, and indeed they disappear from the scene in much the same manner that Nicodemus slipped out of sight in chapter iii. Brown then refers to the "awkwardness" of the whole narrative and suggests that a "poorly known incident from early tradition" was used as the basis for theological adaptation. So he concludes that "there is nothing intrinsically improbable in the basic incident". The issue seems to be not so much in the event itself, whether it happened, as Brown suggests; but rather in the theological significance of the narrative. In a certain sense, the present story is also a sign as well as a paradigmatic event with a profound theological meaning and

---

[13] Raymond E. Brown, *The Gospel according to John,* Vol I (London: Geoffrey Chapman, 1971), p.470

message. The Greeks from Galilee had come to Jerusalem to worship in the Temple. Their option to transcend their loyalty to their own religion and their readiness to appreciate the religious worship of Judaism in Jerusalem enabled them to see a new meaning in the very religiosity of the person of Jesus of Nazareth. At the same time, being Gentiles, they had their own fear whether Jesus would welcome them or not. So they sought the advice of Philip, who in turn contacted Andrew, and both of them went to Jesus to propose the request of the Greeks. The initial reaction of Jesus to the whole scene constitutes the central message of the story. Jesus said: "The hour has come for the Son of Man to be glorified" (John 12:23). For John, glory is not merely the final exaltation of Jesus through his resurrection; rather it is the glory of his passion and death leading to resurrection. Hence the passion is the beginning of that glorification as well as the moment of his being lifted up from the basically earthly and the human. So the passion was for Jesus a moment of transcending the limitations of his human and earthly condition, which for him was his being a Jew with all that it meant for any Jew. Jesus did not want that Jewishness in any manner to become a limiting and controlling factor as well as stumbling block for his elevated and transformed human nature to operate beyond the barriers of his own religion. Jesus had demonstrated this transcendence of several occasions during his earthly ministry, as is clear from the several sayings and stories in the Gospels. Here at the last stage of his earthly ministry Jesus has reached the decisive moment, the real hour. Thereby he was trying to reach out to every human person beyond the barriers of caste, colour and creed.[14] The coming of the Greeks provided this decisive opportunity for Jesus to demonstrate his radical attitude towards religious identity.

It is this inner liberation of Jesus that is explained through the parable of the grain of wheat falling into the earth and dying and thereby giving life and vitality to a new plant growing out of it which bears much fruit (John 12:24). A grain of wheat that refuses to die remains alone and in course of time it loses itself; whereas a grain that is ready to part with its individualized existence becomes a source of life for many other grains. It is interesting to note that Jesus took this example from the nature around us and through that he wants to show that it is something

---

[14] Cf. Joseph Pathrapankal, "Jesus and the Greeks: Reflections on a Theology of Religious Identity" in *Critical and Creative: Studies in Bible and Theology* (Bangalore: Dharmaram Publications, 1986) pp. 71-84.

basic to the very law of nature. Likewise Jesus demonstrated his readiness to die to his own Jewishness in order to become available also to the Gentiles who came in search of him. It is this death which Jesus later explains in terms of his being lifted up from the earth (John 12:32). It is clear that this daring approach to one's own identity is against the basic tendency of all humans because all want to love their life and every aspect of life, whether it is cultural, religious or social. The result is that ultimately they all lose the very life they want to safeguard. But those who are ready to part with the many selfish concerns of life will discover that through their very losing them, they arrive at the meaning of life at a higher level. This is precisely what Jesus did for himself and thereby he established a new attitude towards one's life and identity for the whole humankind. This is the meaning of the saying of Jesus after the parable of the grain of wheat: "Whoever serves me must follow me, and where I am, there will my servant be also" (John 12:26). Jesus wants all those who follow him to be ready for such a *kenosis*. All those who claim to be the disciples of Jesus must have the courage to transcend the limitations and particularities of their identity, including social, cultural or even religious. But it is a very challenging and demanding step for Jesus and it is so for all humans. So John 12:27 gives us a glimpse into a new situation of the personality of Jesus, as he was getting ready to face the hour of his passion and death. Jesus said: "Now my soul is troubled. And what should I say – 'Father, save me from this hour? No, it is for this reason that I have come to this hour'" (John 12:27). It means that Jesus was visibly disturbed and confused about his fate; he was troubled in his innermost reality. He was tempted to say 'No' to the Father. No less than in the Synoptics, the Johannine Jesus is also fearful in the face of the awful struggle of the hour of his passion and death which he was going to face. Jesus struggles with the temptation to cry out to his Father to save him from that hour. But all on a sudden he triumphs and overcome the temptation by submitting himself to the Father's total plans.

The story of Jesus and the Greeks, which we have analysed above, is not just one story among the many others which constitute the earthly ministry of Jesus. It is rather a symbolic and paradigmatic story which has a message for every religious person, especially for Christians living in multi-religious contexts. The attitude the members of a religion should have towards their own religion and towards the followers of other religions is symbolically presented in the attitude of Jesus towards the Greeks. In the prevailing context of Jews avoiding, depreciating and even hating the Gentiles, Jesus sets the example of reaching out to the Greeks and accepting them as fellow pilgrims in the journey of life. Consequently, this story with its inner message can serve as a corrective to some passages in the Bible which have in the past very much prompted the Christians to develop a negative attitude towards the members of other religions, such as 1 Corinthians 10:20-21 and 2 Cor 6:14-18. It is clear that the context in which the author of the Fourth Gospel wrote this story did not have this additional significance it now has in our multi-religious situations. As we have established earlier, beyond the author meaning of a biblical text, it can also have a reader meaning, especially during these times when we have to live within the growing context of religious pluralism. It is becoming more and more clear that religious pluralism is a fact belonging to the very plan of God, which is to be accepted and respected by all.[15] The ever-growing religious pluralism in the world is a blessing and a challenge, and not a burden we have to put up with.

It is this plus-meaning of a text which we could call a *dhvani*-meaning, to borrow a classical Sanskrit expression. *Dhvani* denotes a meaning through evocation, a meaning of resonance, a depth meaning which can be better experienced than expressed. It is a 'third eye' through which one can see the transcending meaning of a text. The readers have to possess a special evocative quality by which they are attuned to this dimension of the text. It is the discovery of a relational order in the realm of meaning. This approach to the Bible is based on the conviction that the Word of God committed to writing is something living and active, and that it can penetrate into every subtle area of the human reality and open new horizons of meanings as it encounters new historical and cultural situations (Heb 4:12). In order to arrive at this in-depth meaning there must emerge a new dialogue between the reader and the text, by which a new contextualized and situative meaning arises, namely, a meaning that is not against the author-meaning and the text-meaning, rather a meaning beyond and above them. It is the result of a creative and dialogical encounter between the readers and the text. Thereby the text begins to speak anew to the readers, and the readers react to the claims of truth made on them by the text. Consequently, there

---

[15] "The religious life of mankind from now on, if it is to be lived at all, will be lived in a context of religious pluralism", Paul F. Knitter, *No Other Name?* (New York: Orbis Books, 985) pp.2-7: Cf. W.C.Smith, *The Faith of the Other Men*, (New York: Harper Row, 1981) p.11.

is a mutual and reciprocal openness of the readers and the text. The text is open to the questions the readers pose and the readers are open to the truth claim of the text. This truth is the further illustration of the basic meaning of the text as was intended by the author.[16]

A New Focus on Christology

The above reflections about how Jesus of Nazareth understood his own religious identity as a Jew and how he was prepared to transcend it for the sake of a better and greater cause of the kingdom of God invite us to develop a new attitude and approach to the question of how we have to understand the whole question of Christian doctrine of the uniqueness and universality of Christ. The ongoing confrontation among theologians between the traditional Christian approach to the significance of Christ in terms of exclusivism and the newly developed concepts of inclusivism and pluralism have contributed very little for a meaningful Christology. The attempts made by some theologians and the official teaching of the Churches to focus on biblical passages, such as Acts 4:12 and 1 Tim 2:5, where the uniqueness and universality of Christ for salvation are positively affirmed, do not lead to any meaningful conclusion because they are faith proclamations of the early believers and not metaphysical statements.[17] It seems that the real significance of Christ is to be discussed not in an apologetic manner as a defense of faith in relation to other religions but rather as a doctrine having its own basis and rationale in the writings of the New Testament, which are the primary documents of our knowledge about Christ. The Gospels and the other writings of the New Testament present the significance of Jesus Christ from a perspective of experience which their writers inherited from the early Christian communities. This experience is based on the fact that Jesus was totally committed to the cause of the kingdom of God with its universal perspectives, a commitment which he sealed through his death and resurrection. It is this universal and transcendent aspect of the message preached by Jesus and understood by his immediate

---

[16] Cf. Paul Ricoeur, *Interpretation Theory: Discourse and the Surplus Meaning* (Forth Worth: Texas Christian University Press, 1976) pp. 29-37.

[17] Cf .Joseph Pathrapankal, "The Significance of Jesus Christ in the Context of Religious Pluralism: A Biblical Critique" in Errol D'Lima and Max Gonsalves (ed) *What does Jesus Christ Mean? The Meaningfulness of Jesus Christ amid Religious Pluralism in India* (Bangalore: NBCLC 1999) pp.107-137.

followers that stands at the centre of the New Testament kerygma. Jesus of Nazareth had to broaden the horizons of the religious thinking that was current in Judaism and also among other henotheistic religious traditions of his times.

What Paul F. Knitter has formulated about the whole issue of Christological discussions in our times seems to offer a healthy approach to Christology in the context of religious pluralism: "If Christians, trusting in God and respecting the faith of others, engage in this new encounter with other traditions, they can expect to witness a growth or evolution such as Christianity has not experienced since its first centuries. This growth will paradoxically both preserve the identity of Christianity and at the same time transform it. Such paradox is no mystery; we are acquainted with it in our personal lives as well as in nature".[18] It seems that the defenders of the absolute uniqueness of Christ are somehow victims of what L. Swidler calls a kind of 'boastful hybris' creeping into Christian claims of superiority. As opposed to it, what Jesus presents about his personality is his ultimate *kenosis*. The true meaning of Christ's *kenosis* is not that he was first divine and then he became human in order once again to regain his divinity (Phil 2:6-11). The basic issue is that Jesus of Nazareth also rejected that kind of humanity which refuses to empty itself, so that by becoming perfectly selfless and altruistic he could become the instrument of God's compassion and love for the whole humankind.[19]

The parable discourse of Jesus in the Gospel of Mathew concludes with a question raised by Jesus to his disciples: "Did you understand all these?" meaning thereby the obscure and subtle things he said about the nature of the kingdom of God through illustrations and parabolic language. "Yes", they said to him, even if they did not understand everything they had heard. In fact, during this long discourse consisting of a series of seven parables about the kingdom of God, after the first parable of the sower and the parable of the weeds, Jesus had to spend time to explain to his disciples the inner meaning of these parables. Now after all the parables have been presented, the disciples are in a position to say that they have understood them. Then Jesus went to make a solemn comment about his disciples, about what they should be in so

---

[18] Paul F. Knitter, *No Other Name?* (New York: Orbis Books, 1985) p.230.

[19] Cf. J. S. Samartha, *One Christ-Many Religions* (New York: Orbis Books, 1991) p. 155.

far as they are his disciples, not only at the time he was speaking to his immediate disciples but also his disciples for all times in the mission he entrusted to the Church. He said: "Every scribe who has been trained for the kingdom of heaven is like the master of a household who brings out of his treasure what is new and what is old" (Matt 13:51-52). The disciples are called 'scribes trained for the kingdom of heaven'; they are said to be 'householders'; they should have a 'treasure' with them; they are also entitled to bring 'what is new and what is old' from that treasure. It would appear that in this statement of Mathew we have the picture of true biblical exegetes for our times who know how to deal with issues within the larger framework of the kingdom of God for which they are trained and to which they have to remain committed.

The evangelist Mathew is said to be a theologian in his own right in so far as he was an authentic representative of the 'School of Mathew' which undertook the major task of presenting the gospel of Jesus of Nazareth from a didactic and pastoral perspective for the community of the Palestinian Jewish Christians after it had to break away from the official Judaism of the first century. The evangelist has taken special care to show that Jesus of Nazareth is the expected Messiah and the Emmanuel who came to fulfill the Torah and Prophets and not to destroy them (Matt 5:17). At the same time, he was convinced that the gospel which Jesus of Nazareth announced was not a mere continuation of the Torah and the Prophets, that an entirely new reality has dawned in history which has now to control and guide the entire thinking pattern and life style of all humans, irrespective of to what colour, caste and creed they belonged. This is what Jesus announced as the kingdom of God, which is God's ultimate and definitive gift to humanity and it was presented as something reaching the humankind on the verge of the fulfillment of time (Matt 4:17). Jesus proposed a new criterion and a new requirement on the part of his hearers to belong to this new situation, namely, a new *dharma* (Matt 5:20) that exceeded that of the Jewish leaders of his time. It is the ongoing articulation of this new *dharma* that should enable the exegetes and theologians of our times to discover anew the old and the new and see them in relation to the contemporary situations and their reference and relevance to their life and ministry.

VI

RELIGIOUS MAXIMS AS SHAPING HISTORY
A STUDY ON MATTHEW 5:48

The amazing and tremendous role words play in our daily life, the place they hold and the power they wield, are astonishingly great. The very quantity of words, both spoken and written, throughout the world during the course of a day is astonishing. They issue from minds, pass through hearts and mouths of men and women, from swift pens of gifted people and from busy editorial offices, homes, schools, market-places, assemblies, parliaments and international meetings. The function of human words is diverse; but it is basically vital, having dynamic powers with them. Words are also functional and foundational, for instance, in the education of children. They are built up with words, and much of their specifically human growth is secured through words. Without words and language there would be little or nothing that can be achieved through education, social life, personal encounter, international communication and human development. A great deal of our life is made up of words, speech and language, and they lie deep in the foundations of civilization. The more perfect, developed and refined the word is, the greater is its power to express, to educate and also to effect. The more powerful the speech, the nearer it comes to action. Wars and peace accords are decided by words, uttered or written. Words can wound and heal, kill and create, destroy things and build them up, confuse issues and enlighten them. A word can disrupt a friendship that was built up through many years, it undermine self-confidence, it can also ruin lives and cause conflagrations within families and nations. A word can also soothe the sorrowing heart, infuse confidence and rebuild broken lives and kindle dying love. Words can cheer, comfort, console. They can inspire, create, attract and persuade. Words can stimulate creative thinking and carry ideas across ages and oceans. Such is the human word, and it is a mysterious thing, beautiful and terrible, frail and effective, flexible and firm, moulding us while it is being moulded by us.[1]

In fact, human word is a profound mystery of this sort because basically it is the symbol, the sign and image of the divine word, which transcends and controls all human words. God's word is all these and much more, and it operates at the deepest levels of human existence, in the very

---

[1] Cf. Samuel Rayan, "The Word of God" *Jeevadhara* 1(1971) 96-97.

heart of human life. A New Testament author wrote about the power of the word of God: "The word of God is living and active, sharper than any two-edged sword, piercing until it divides soul from spirit, joints from marrow; it is able to judge the thoughts and intentions of the heart" (Heb 4:12). Men and women were chosen by God to utter this word of God and they experienced the power of this word for their own life and for their entire mission. To the prophet Jeremiah the word was a gift given by God, imparting energy for action and infusing strength to endure in the midst of the challenges he had to face. He was set over nations and kingdoms to speak up and act: "to pluck up and to pull down, to destroy and to overthrow, and then to build and to plant" (Jer 1:10). Prophet Isaiah was given the task of announcing the creative and effective nature of the word of God. He wrote: "As the rain and the snow come down from heaven, and do not return there until they have watered the earth, making it bring forth and sprout, giving seed to the sower and bread to the eater, so shall my word be that goes out from my mouth; it shall not return to me empty, but it shall accomplish that which I purpose, and succeed in the thing for which I sent it" (Isa 55:10-11). The word of God that was sent to Mary through the angel Gabriel was accepted by her as the controlling power of her life and at a later date Jesus pronounced his blessings on Mary on account of her commitment to that word (Lk 11:27-28).

All religions have their own ways of articulating the divine dimension of the word. The religion of Israel reflected on the meaning of word through its Hebrew equivalent *dabar,* which was understood as the manifestation and externalization of a person. In the Ancient Near East the spoken word was conceived of as a distinct reality laden with power. This was particularly true of the divine word. In both Egypt and Mesopotamia the divine word was a creative force bringing the world into existence. The belief in the power of the word seems to reflect a pre-literary culture in which there were no written records to preserve the spoken word. The spoken word was an externalization of the persons, which was supposed to outlive the persons themselves. The word posits a reality; this reality first exists in the mind and heart, then it passes into speech, and finally the effective speech brings into existence the reality that it signifies. In this conception, the power of the word is rooted in the persons themselves. When the persons speak, they externalize themselves through the words that are uttered. The permanence and energy of personal volition reach the external world through the spoken word, and the spoken word retains and exercises these qualities of permanence and energy. In the case of the word of God it does not always realize itself all on a sudden. Once uttered, the word is posited outside of God in human history. It will infallibly realize itself, and the full reality will be that designated by the word. The word of

God is the nerve and hinge of biblical history taken as a whole. The various narratives which constitute the Old Testament and New Testament history are linked together by this co-ordinating theme of the word of God. It is within the framework of this word that the entire Bible is written. As a collection of events, all controlled and regulated by the word of God, the Bible is called the word of God, the written record of the accomplished word of God in history. As the *dabar* of God, as word, thing and event, the word of God in the Bible is the concrete and written form of the words and deeds of God which constitute God's revelation and action in history.

It is this word of God in and through history which still continues to confront and challenge humans in various forms in our times. It confronts us in the form of the written word in the Bible, in the Vedas, in the Dhammapada and the Sutta Pithaka, in the Qur'an, in the Guru Grandh Sahib with its saving, challenging, encouraging and consoling dimensions. It is the duty of all religious-minded persons to turn to this multifaceted word and try to derive inspiration and nourishment from it for the success of the journey of their life, irrespective of to which religion they belong. In this study we are trying to present the enlightening and challenging message of a specific saying of Jesus Christ in the Sermon on the Mount, which has within it some of the most demanding and inspiring ideas of an elevated humanism and we try to see this saying as a *Mahavakya*, a Great Saying, through which Jesus wanted to give to his hearers a message which should guide their life as a whole. Though the expression *Mahavakya* has a restricted meaning in Hinduism, here we use the concept in a rather wider sense in so far as it can be attributed to significant and enriching sayings which have an application to the relationship between God and humans, between humans and their society as well as the humans in their relationship to the cosmos as a whole. Before we proceed with our study of this *Mahavakya* of Jesus Christ it is important that we analyse the various components of the very concept of *Mahavakya* in order to understand its inner nuances, whether it is in Hinduism or in Christianity or in any other religion. There are some inherent concepts underlying the concept of *Mahavakya,* such as *Vak* and *Vakya* and all these concepts are inter-related and inter-connected.

The Nuances of *Vak, Vakya* and *Mahavakya*

The Sanskrit word *vāk*, meaning 'word', is derived from the verbal root '*vac*' (*vakti*), which means 'to say', 'to tell', 'to relate' 'to describe' and 'to announce'. The expression *vakya* is derived from *vak,* and it means 'speech', 'sentence' 'utterance of a thought'. Brahman, who is pure existence and pure consciousness, manifests itself as the *vak* and the initial creative vibration and breath in Brahman was *vak*. This word exists in four forms in a descending order: *para vak, pasyanti vak, madhyama vak* and the *vaikahari vak*. *Para vak* is the absolute, supreme, highest word which exists only in the inner essence of the supreme, un-manifested Brahman. In a way it is the supreme Brahman itself. The *pasyanti vak* is the word in creation, the first manifestation of Brahman, which has the cosmic form. The *madhyama vak* is manifested to the mind of the sages and saints in meditation through *sruti*. *Sruti* is revealed to and is heard by the sages in this word. The *vaikhari vak* is that word which can be heard and understood by ordinary humans. Revelation is transmitted to humanity in this word. We can find parallels to this approach to the word in Christian theology also. In his teaching on the Book of Psalms Martin Luther, the reformer of the Church, speaks about four levels of the word (*logos*). The topmost level is the inner word, which exists only in the supreme Lord as his eternal power. This word becomes manifest in space and time in an external word, which is Jesus Christ. The third level of the word is the word of God in the Bible because the Bible contains the history of God's communication with the humanity. The fourth level of the word is the living word of the Bible operating in and through humans. It is through their words and deeds that humans have to reveal the living word of God.

Consequently, the word is eternally identified with Brahman and it is Brahman itself, and it willed to pronounce and reproduce itself in space and time in the beginning of each cycle of time. Thus this eternal word became *sruti*, which is communicated to and heard by the sages. But something is positively heard only if it is uttered and given phonetic expression. Hence the sages transmitted the word further. Honest utterance of the word also manifests the inner nature of the speaker. Thus the word, that is first of all uttered by God and that is later on heard by worthy humans, ultimately manifests the inner nature of Brahman. This is the process of the revelation of God to the humankind. Applying these notions to the Bible, the Gospel of John also speaks about the word that was in the beginning, the word that was with God, the word that was God (John 1:1). Later on the author speaks about this eternal word which became flesh (John 1:14), which is to be understood as the concrete human reality, and dwelt in this world. It is this word-made-flesh who revealed the inner essence of God through his word, which is known as the preaching and teaching of Jesus Christ. The Gospels contain this word in a variety of forms, many of which have the nature of a *mahavakya,* a great and significant saying which has a profound message with it.

Hence a *mahavakya* is a big sentence, literally, a great *vakya*, which is a convergence of several words, but together they constitute one basic idea and convey one basic message. A *vakya*, to be meaningful and intelligible, must have four qualities. First of all, the words in a sentence are to be inter-related in such a way that they express a coherent and complete idea. A few unrelated words do not make any sense. Secondly, the words should possess the aptness to convey the correct sense and should not express contradictory meaning. Thirdly, the words should be arranged in such a manner that the sentence brings out the idea with a new force. Fourthly, the intention of the speaker must be clear in case there is some ambiguity in the words and power. It is possible that some words have two different meanings. Here the hearers have to make out the meaning of the sentence according to the context and the saying must be such that the context is clear to the hearers. There are linguists and philosophers who say that a sentence is the basic linguistic reality which conveys meaning. Letters and words are mere abstractions form a sentence. Only in the context of a sentence letters and words have their real and fuller meaning. This is particularly true of a *mahavakya*. An analysis of Matthew 5:48, understood as a *mahavakya,* will bring out this truth. Now we try to apply these qualities to an important saying of Jesus of Nazareth which forms the climax of his teaching about Christian discipleship in the Sermon on the Mount.

Background of the *Mahavakya* in Matthew 5:48

The *mahavakya* in Matthew 5:48 comes within the larger framework of what is known as the Sermon on the Mount in the Gospel of Matthew (Matt 5:1-7:28). The Gospels are not the biographies of Jesus Christ. Rather they are a kind of proclamation based on events and happenings which took place during the public ministry of Jesus of Nazareth at a particular time and in a particular place, known as Palestine. The basic quality of this proclamation is that it is 'Good News' for all. In fact, the English word 'Gospel' is derived from the Old English words 'god' and 'spel' , meaning 'good news'. Gospel is the English rendering of the Greek word *euaggelion* and the Latin *evangelium.* Before the Gospels were written during the first century of the Common Era, there was already the gospel preached by Jesus Christ which was understood by his hearers as the Good News announced to them. The four Gospels contain a series of the teachings of Christ and some of them are presented as long discourses. One of these discourses is known as the Sermon on the Mount, which had a tremendous influence on many people in forming and framing their personality in their personal, social and political life. One such great example is Mahatma Gandhi, the Father of the Nation, who spoke about the Sermon on the Mount as something which went "straight into his heart".[2] He has made it clear that he was very much influenced by this teaching of Jesus: "It was the New Testament which really awakened me to the rightness and values of passive resistance. When I read in the Sermon on the Mount such passages as 'Resist not him that is evil'.... I was simply overjoyed". [3] In *Young India* he wrote about the Sermon on the Mount: "It is that Sermon that endeared Jesus to me and even if it is proved that Jesus never lived, still the Sermon on the Mount would be true for me".[4] In his *Message of Jesus Christ* he wrote: "I can say that Jesus occupies in my heart the place of one of the greatest teachers who has made a considerable influence on my life. Leave the Christians alone for the present. I shall say to the Hindus that your lives will be incomplete unless you reverently study the teaching of Jesus".[5] In particular, Matthew 5:38-48 influenced him very much because these verses speak against retaliation and malice, and affirm categorically love and forgiveness as the way of life. There is a story about the British Viceroy, Lord Irvin, during the famous Round Table Conference held in London in 1931, asking Mahatma Gandhi about what he had to propose to solve the longstanding problems between England and India. And Gandhi replied: "The Sermon on the Mount has in it the solution for all the problems in the world. Let us practise it and then there will be peace in the world".

These general observations about the influence of the Sermon on the Mount on Mahatma Gandhi are proof of the importance of its teachings. According to biblical scholars, the Sermon on the Mount is a collection of the teachings of Jesus as it was preserved and made use of in the teaching of the early Christian communities which was later on put into writing through the literary activity of competent persons in those communities. Consequently, this discourse contains important teachings for those who want to improve the quality of their ethical life in relation to God and to the society as a whole. As one who had come to inaugurate a new way of being fully human in the midst of this world, Jesus demanded that all have to be converted and assume new attitudes and ideals in their life. It was not at all question of a conversion from one religion to another; rather it was all about a radical change in one's way of thinking and living. Jesus

---

[2] M.K.Gandhi, *An Autobiography: The Story of My Experience with Truth* in *Selected Works of Mahatma Gandhi*, Vol I (Ahmedabad: Navajivan Publishing House, 1969) p. 101.

[3] Cf. M.K.Gandhi, *Speeches and Writings of Mahatma Gandhi* (Ahmedabad: Navajivan Publishing House, 1959) p. 130.

[4] M.K.Gandhi, *The Message of Jesus Christ*, Anand T. Hingorani (ed) (Bombay: Bharatiya Vidya Bhavan, 1963), p. 66.

[5] M.K.Gandhi, *The Message of Jesus Christ,* p. 144.

wanted all humans to have an inner disposition through which they were exhorted to accept the message he gave them and this is known as a better *dharma,* which was characterized by interiority and inter-personalism. It is not true that Jesus gave all the teaching contained in the Sermon on the Mount in one sitting; rather what he taught on different occasions during his earthly ministry were collected and edited through the theological genius of the early Christian writers, and now we have them in the form of a long sermon. The discourse is introduced with a reference to Jesus going up the mountain and sitting down, when the disciples went near to him and also a big crowd of people gathered around him (Matt 5:1-2). This solemn introduction to the discourse makes it clear that it was an authoritative teaching of Jesus, through which he explained the radical demands for the building up of a healthy society.

The locale of the teaching of Jesus as the mountain is also very important. Sacred mountains and mountain symbolism are common features of all religions, and it was all the more so in the landscape of Israel's religious life from earliest times. The mountainous nature of the land of Palestine - two extended ridges of mountains on both sides of river Jordan valley - added to the importance given to mountain in Israel's religious tradition. Israel shared with her neighbours the significance of mountains, originating from the concept of the cosmic mountain.[6] Here the significance of the mountain is not geographical rather symbolical and theological at the same time. In the same way as God is said to have revealed himself to selected individuals, so also the belief in Israel was that not every place was appropriate for divine revelation, and mountains were supposed to be the fitting places. Mountain was a symbol of divine power and nearness and the site of divine encounters. Mountains are also places from which the great expanses of the universe can be surveyed and consequently they are the apt places for a universal and cosmic vision of realities as we have it in the Sermon on the Mount.

The Context of the *Mahavakya* in Matthew 5:48

The first part of the Sermon on the Mount (Matt 5:3-12) is a collection of greetings and demands, traditionally known as the *beatitudes,* through which the hearers are told about the need of their having some radical dispositions, such as the "poverty of the spirit" (Matt 5:3) in order to benefit from the teaching of Jesus. Only those who are aware of their own limitations and are prepared to depend on God are privileged to enter into the meaning of the teaching of Jesus. The expression 'poverty of the spirit'

---

[6] Cf.J.Clifford, *The Cosmic Mountain in Canaan and the Old Testament: Harvard Semitic Monographs 4* (Cambridge: Harvard University Press, 1972) pp. 9-25.

needs closer examination. Whereas the word 'spirit' can mean the supreme *Brahman* as well as the participated *atman*, it can also mean the centre of human self-awareness and self-understanding, which either tends to affirm itself through *ahamkara* or to assume an attitude of humility and honest recognition of one's own limitation. It is this latter group which can be called 'poor in spirit'. They are humble, honest and simple, and are not sophisticated and calculating in their dealings with others. The entire Sermon on the Mount is addressed to such people because they are ready to listen to God. Hence the *beatitudes* are salutations and invitations at the same time, through which the hearers are invited to enjoy the blessings of the new situation Jesus was inaugurating in the society of his times. These people are addressed as meek, as merciful and pure in heart, as those who hunger and thirst for *dharma*. It is also the teaching of Jesus that such people will be persecuted for the cause of *dharma*. Their readiness to suffer for the cause of the gospel and reign of God will eventually entitle them to the blessings of God (Matt 5:11-12).

Jesus had a tremendous capacity to observe the realities of the world around him. For him the nature was a open book with a variety of lessons to be culled from it. The lilies of the field and the birds of the air are for him manifestations of the divine and they can carry a great message for his hearers (Matt 6:25-33). He was very much fascinated by the seed that was scattered on the ground which would sprout and grow and eventually become a plant bearing flowers and fruits (Mark 4:26-29). He would look at salt, the cheapest commodity available in the market, and teach great lessons about the quality of the persons who would follow his teaching. He says: "You are the salt of the earth" (Matt 5:13-14). Salt is one of the most indispensable things for maintaining our earthly life and it is also the most available thing in the market. It is this salt that gives taste to food, preserves things from decaying and has the medical quality of healing the wounds. But to accomplish these tasks the salt has to dissolve and at the same time preserve its basic saltness. It is all a process of losing and gaining, a process of involvement and transcendence, a process of death and life. The same idea is brought out in the following saying of Jesus: "You are the light of the world.... Let your light shine before others, so that they may see your good works and give glory to your Father in heaven" (Matt 5:15-16). In the same way as an oil lamp burns and gives light to all in the family, the disciples of Jesus must burn by themselves and give light and brightness to the whole human community and to the whole created universe. Here it is a question of self-emptying and an exercise of altruism that is characteristic of the lamp which burns in order to give light to others.

In Matthew 5:16 Jesus analyses a special dimension of being and doing through which his disciples have to be the light of the world. They should always perform good works (*kala erga*) in their day-to-day life and thereby enable people to praise their Father who is in heaven. There is a lot of meaning stored in the expression "good works". The followers of Jesus have to reveal their being the light of the world through their good actions, namely, actions through which they convey goodness and beauty. There are two words in Greek which can be translated 'good': *agathos* and *kalos*. Whereas the qualifying adjective *agathos* means something that is ethically good, the adjective *kalos* means something that is not only ethically but also aesthetically good. The meaning of what Jesus said is that the actions of his followers should be not only ethically, but also aesthetically good, something befitting their being the children of God. Jesus was not a puritan. He wanted his disciples to be normal citizens of this world who are refined in the exercise of their religion. All that is done in the name of spirituality with a kind of other-worldly austerity and rigour, because of which many people develop a kind of allergy to things divine and spiritual, is not according to the mind of Jesus.

The Inner Content of the *Mahavakya* in Matthew 5:48: "Be Mature as your heavenly Father is Mature"

The central theme of the Sermon on the Mount is the invitation to practise a new and better *dharma* which Jesus demands from his hearers as a requirement for belonging to the new religious situation. Jesus inaugurated this new situation with the concept of the kingdom of God. Although the expression 'kingdom of God' carries with it an archaic concept smacking the ancient outmoded style of kings and kingdoms, in the teaching of Jesus this concept is very important. First of all, the kingdom of God in the preaching of Jesus is not to be understood spatially, but operationally. The Kingdom of God means God's sovereign activity and a quality of existence as well as a state of being in which God exercises his divine reign. It is a concept related to the creation of the world and its sustenance. Jesus presented this concept in terms of the definitive coming of God to the humankind to establish his full and unimpeded care over the world. The most important aspect of the concept of the kingdom of God in the preaching of Jesus is that he never refers to God as the king but as the *abba, the Father,* who cares for all his children and wants them to have full trust and confidence in him. It is this picture of the Father[7] which Jesus tries to emphasize throughout the Sermon

---

[7] *Abba* is the Aramaic word for 'father'. Through this expression 'father' attributed to God no attempt is made to continue the patriarchal language of our traditional theology. In the absence of a better word we still have to use the conventional one trying to see in it aspects of Father and Mother, who

on the Mount. It is from this concept of God as the Father of the entire cosmos that all relations take on a new meaning and a new dynamism, which transcend case, colour and creed. For Jesus God is the Father, all are God's children and among themselves all are sisters and brothers. This universalism is basic and central to Jesus' teaching about the kingdom of God and it is also the major matrix within which we have to understand the uniqueness of his teaching as a whole. It seems that Jesus took over this concept of the kingdom from the Old Testament precisely to charge and fill it with these important ideas about the personal dimensions of the new religious and social situation he came to inaugurate and establish.

The teaching of Jesus about the kingdom of God with its new personal dimensions is to be seen in relation to Jesus' vision of a new society which lies at the basis of his entire preaching and teaching. During the ministry of Jesus Judaism was very much a ghetto religion that was preoccupied only with its own well-being. The Jewish teachers of the law could see only the other Jew as their neighbours and so they taught others. The temple of Jerusalem with its divisions into the court of the Jews, the court of women and the court of the Gentiles was a symbol of this divided and discriminated humanity. Even in Judaism there existed many sects, often one opposed to the other, having its own ideologies and idiosyncrasies. More than that, the vast majority of the people, known as the *am haarez*, meaning the people of the land, were a marginalized group because they were called 'sinners' on account of their lack of expertise in the understanding of the Law of Moses and their commitment to the observance of the particulars of these regulations. The Jews had even the custom of addressing the followers of other religions as 'dogs'. Such attitudes and practices were symptomatic of a society that was characterized by its hatred and lack of respect for all others who were not Jews. In the context of this exaggerated polarization in the society of his times Jesus wanted to inaugurate the beginnings of a new society on the basis of a radical conversion which the people had to effect at the level of mind and heart. The inner meaning of this conversion was not only a spiritual preparation; rather it meant also the challenge of accepting new values and new attitudes to life and to persons. Jesus wanted to build up a society that would abolish all categories of discrimination between economic and ethnic groups. What was basic to this new approach was the creation of interpersonal relationship as the hallmark of the new society.

The immediate background of the *mahavakya* we are analysing here is related to the discussion on the six antitheses in the realm of

---

are symbols of love, care and concern. In a certain sense the attempt made by some religions to present a Mother God is a salutary sign of this holistic approach to divinity.

interpersonal relationship, through which Jesus tries to throw light on the various dimensions of the new *dharma*, which he wants his hearers to put into practice in order to articulate the inner reality of their new life. There are six cases which contrast what was hitherto taught and practised with what Jesus now teaches his hearers to learn from him and then put into practice in their day-to-day life in order to make their life authentic and meaningful. The primary function of this discussion is to show what sort of attitude and behaviour Jesus expects from his hearers and how his demands surpass those of the law of Moses without in any way contradicting the spirit of the same law. What is important to observe here is how Jesus goes into the inner, deeper and comprehensive meaning of the new *dharma*. All the six antitheses deal with cases of interpersonal relationship because the essence of religion as understood by Jesus is built up on the reality of radical relationship based on the Fatherhood of God. From this basic truth all aspects of human relationship in the society have to follow. It is to highlight this fundamental teaching that Jesus selected six representative areas of interpersonal relationship, through which Jesus teaches and challenges his hearers. In fact, interpersonal relationship is an area in which most of the problems of community life in family as well as in the society take their origin and create problems. If this was true in ancient times, it is all the more applicable to our times, because the whole world has now emerged as a global village and communications are taking place very fast which either foster relationship or destroy it.

The *mahavakya* in Matthew 5:48 is the crowning statement of Jesus after he had given the blueprint of a better society in which interpersonal relationship is to be of a higher quality and nobility. To establish this doctrine Jesus takes up several cases of interpersonal issues. Accordingly, not only murder is ethically wrong but also all forms of violating the reputation and integrity of fellow-humans (Matt 5:21-22). So also, not only adultery is a sin action, but also all external and internal actions through which others are made the objects of one's own selfish lust (Matt 5:27-32). The followers of Jesus are also exhorted to be honest, sincere and truthful in all what they say without their having recourse to swearing, because swearing is a subtle attempt to escape the transparency in one's own character (Matt 5:33-37). All must realize that their spoken words are the concrete expressions of their inner personality. Every human utterance is a sacred transaction with others. The Code of Hammurabi, the sixth king of the first dynasty of Babylon (BCE 1728-1686), had prescribed a restrictive law regarding vengeance: "An eye for an eye and a tooth for a tooth", and thereby it meant that retaliation must not in any manner exceed the wrong done. This law was developed in a culture where a spirit of revenge was leading people to all kinds of atrocities. In the place of this Jesus told his disciples that they should completely rise above the spirit of retaliation and do things in a different manner, which would cost them very much. The question is one of overcoming evil with goodness and of creating a new order of mature and noble behaviour among people (Matt 5:38-42). It is not at all a call to passivity and a promotion of the prevailing principle in the contemporary society: "might is right". Rather than demanding strict justice or allowing for retaliation of any kind, the disciples of Jesus have to give deference to others, even if they become losers.

After he has explained five areas of interpersonal relationship, Jesus takes up the sixth and the most challenging realm of interpersonal relationship, namely, the invitation to the love of enemies (Matt 5:43-47). This is the climactic teaching about the new *dharma* which is to be practised by the followers of Jesus. Once again Jesus transcends the barriers and limitations of caste, colour and creed in this teaching. It is noteworthy that here Jesus rises above the conventional distinction between the good and the evil as well as the righteous and the unrighteous. The simple reason for this new approach to all is that here it is question of the overarching reality of the Fatherhood of God which brings together all humans into the same framework of a new family of interpersonal relationship. In this last antithesis the contrast of what was practised so far and what is taught by Jesus as well as the two imageries of the rain and the sun used by him to illustrate his point make it one of the most challenging doctrines of the Bible. Its presence also in the Gospel of Luke (Luke 6:27-28; 32-34) with minor differences points to the authentic origin of this teaching of Jesus in the early Christian tradition.

In the Old Testament there was a positive law that the people of Israel should love their neighbours (Lev 19:18). But there was no such law they should hate their enemies. It was more a practice than a positive law. Though hatred of enemies was not taught in the Old Testament, it was something that was being practised among the people of Israel. The law about the love of neighbour naturally raised the question as to who a neighbour was. For Israel, in general, and for the Jews, at the time Jesus, neighbours were the other Jews, whether they lived next door or in some other place. Consequently, the followers of other religions who lived next door to the Jews were not considered as neighbours. As the law of Moses prescribed only the love of neighbour, the practice arose of not loving the followers of other religions, which naturally turned out to hating and disliking them. A clear evidence of this hatred as a sectarian doctrine and practice is found in the *Manual of Discipline,* where every member of the

Essene community of Qumran[8] was asked to make his task to love all the members of the community and to hate all the outsiders, as the latter group was considered as constituting the children of darkness.[9]

For Jesus all such considerations are to be avoided. His disciples have to love even the so-called 'enemies'. They have to pray for those who persecute them. Through this extreme demand Jesus brings the issue of loving the enemies to a painful and challenging experience. By demanding this love of enemies Jesus was not referring to some abstract and dry attitude towards them, through which the disciples overcome their ill-feelings towards such people; rather it demands undergoing the challenging exercise of praying for them, for their well-being and for their success in life, which is psychologically and emotionally a very difficult exercise. Jesus himself did it on the cross when he prayed for those who crucified him (Lk 23:34). He also gave his disciples this directive as a new commandment, as a command of mutual love and exhorted them to love each other as he himself had loved them (John 13:34-35). It means a universal love, a love that was extended even to the one who betrayed him. It is a love that costs and also a love that hurts the one who loves. Through this teaching Jesus set the tone of a universal brotherhood and sisterhood of all people, a new situation of mutuality and co-operation. The teaching of Jesus is very clear; it is very authoritative and radical. It is a demand which he places before his disciples which they have to follow at all costs.

The reasons why the disciples have to come up to this high ideal of interpersonal relationship is demonstrated through the close relationship they have to their Father in heaven who is very generous and magnanimous towards all. The children have to act like the Father who does not have any ill-feelings towards his children, irrespective of their being good or evil, righteous or unrighteous. This the Father does not only in giving his invisible grace to them but also through his day-to-day gifts of rain and sun. In sending his rain and making his sun rise on this planet earth, God never shows any partiality or stinginess. He is generous to the maximum. Hence the children also should have the same attitude of the Father as their own. If they love and greet only those who love and greet them in return, they are far removed from the true ideals of discipleship. It is precisely what the so-called outcasts, such as the tax collectors, the sinners and the Greeks do. It could also be that sometimes they are far better disciples than the so-called

---

[8] Excavations at Khirbet Qumran near to the Dead Sea in Israel from 1947 onwards have revealed that a religious group of Jews lived here who had their own religious convictions and practices. The community was destroyed by the Romans during their siege on Jerusalem Ce 68-70.

[9] Cf. 1QS 1:1-15; 9:21-26.

disciples of Jesus who have not yet learned how to overcome their basic sentimentality and spirit of contempt towards others.

What Jesus has to give through this teaching about the love of enemies is perhaps the most difficult and demanding for the disciples to put into practice. Hence Jesus expects from them a conscious and willful action and not one that is spontaneous and natural to them. It is not a question of a feeling; rather it is a matter of rising above the level of feeling and doing things in a noble and mature manner. The Greek verb used here is *agapao*, which means a noble and mature love. It is not the kind of love between parents and children or between the children in a natural family; nor is it the kind of love that is experienced between like-minded people, which is very often warm and affectionate. *Agape* is the result of a benevolent, elevated and noble conviction and an invincible and unconquerable good will. The origin of this conviction is in what Jesus has taught about the universal Fatherhood of God and the universal sisterhood and brotherhood of all human persons. Based on that conviction, the disciples have to take a firm decision to consider all others as their brothers and sisters, no matter how their attitude is, no matter how they are treated by them in return. It needs constant and abiding courage to have this conviction and consequent attitude maintained and refreshed, which no disciple may succeed in practising for long unless they are supported by the power of God and by a strong will. The disciples must realize their own weakness and ask for the continuous support and guidance of the Father in this demanding area of life. They must rely on the power of the spirit who alone can enable the disciples to abide by their convictions and commitment. It is part of the poverty of the spirit, to which the disciples were invited as the primary condition for entering the kingdom of God. What is of great significance in this teaching of Jesus is how he transcends the parameters of religion and religious principles through his reference to the phenomena of the nature, such as rain and sun, as the great teachers of religious wisdom. Through this daring approach Jesus tries to show that religion is not a parochial reality concerned with some esoteric principles meant for a group of people initiated into them; but rather the healthy articulation of the very human nature.

Jesus goes on to say: "Be perfect (*teleioi*), therefore, as your heavenly Father is perfect (*teleios*) (Matt 5:48). To anyone reading this passage the first reaction would be: Can we ever become perfect like the heavenly Father? God, the Father, is above all and he is all holy, and humans are mere creatures, limited and sinners. Is it that Jesus through this exhortation is showing us an impossible ideal in such a way that in the face of this difficult goal we become aware of our helplessness and thereby entrust ourselves to God in total resignation? Some theologians in the past have tried to interpret the teaching of Jesus in this manner. But it seems that here there is no such question of an impossible ideal. Rather the issue discussed here is not of an abstract ideal of perfection to be practised by humans. Matthew 5:48 begins this verse with a `therefore' (*oun*), which means that it is the conclusion as well as an application of what was discussed above. There Jesus had shown the example of God, the Father, who in his generosity, goodness and maturity is sending his rain on the good and the bad alike, and is making his sun rise on the righteous and the unrighteous. This was precisely to demonstrate to his disciples the need of loving the neighbours and the enemies equally without any discrimination. God loves all, cares for all. This is the ideal and example that is to be followed by all humans in so far they are God's children. They should not be stingy and narrow-minded; rather they have to be generous and large-hearted. If only they realize that these so-called bad people are their own brothers and sisters, they will come out of their ill-feelings and accept them as their brothers and sisters and act accordingly. What is needed here for such an approach is the spirit of the generosity, goodness and maturity of the Father, an ideal the disciples must always keep before their eyes.

Here the word `perfect', the Greek *teleios*, can be better translated as 'mature'. The underlying idea in this teaching is that of human maturity, which means the capacity and artfulness to act in a particular situation that will be appreciated by others. It is not a question of feelings, rather of maturity. Most of the actions people perform are coloured by their emotions and immature feelings and to that extent they very often lack maturity. Biological maturity is something the humans can easily take care of. But intellectual, spiritual, religious, emotional and psychological maturity needs their maximum attention and application and it is necessary to keep it up and develop it for a successful life. It is probable that the Hebrew and Aramaic word which stands behind the Greek *teleios* was *tamim*, which means `simple', `straightforward' and `unsophisticated' in contrast to `complex' `crooked` and `calculating'. If we take this meaning, it is that God the Father is simple in his dealings with the children and not calculating as the humans.[10] What very often happens with humans is that they are all very much scheming and calculating, and thereby interpersonal relationships become complex and complicated. Very often their selfishness and narrow-mindedness are the guiding principles of these calculations in their social life. They divide people into good and bad to suit their own convenience and plans. It is precisely here that the disciples of Jesus should learn to imitate

---

[10] The Hebrew equivalent *tamim* occurs frequently in the Qumran texts; it is also the self-designation of this group which was supposed to walk on the "perfect way" by keeping the rigorously intensified Torah (1 QS 1.8.13 f).

the example of the Father who is simple and large-hearted, straightforward and generous. It seems the same meaning is emphasized by Luke also in his Sermon on the Plain, where we read: "Be merciful as also your Father is merciful" (Luke 6:36). To be merciful *(oiktirmon)* is a quality of God through which he forgets and forgives the misgivings of his children. God is not hard-hearted and cruel. So also the children have to be kind and merciful. In the same way as all expect others to be kind and understanding towards them, so they also have to be considerate and kind to others. In a world characterized by an aggressive and consumerist culture, it is the duty of the disciples of Jesus to be altruistic, kind and merciful to others.

Hence the perfection and maturity of the Father are not an impossible ideal set before the disciples, but models and patterns of behaviour which they have to put into practice every moment of their life. It follows that perfection is not a special status of a few people, as if there is a state of perfection to which some are called. What is imperative in our passage is the preparedness of the disciples to rise above their selfish feelings through which they keep those whom they do not like outside of their consideration and concern. Rather, looking at the mature, simple and kind attitude of the Father, they have to develop a more mature and merciful behaviour in their interpersonal relationship. With this concluding statement in 5:48, Matthew finally directs the teaching of the six antitheses back to God himself. He is perfect, simple and kind, and Matthew names him "your heavenly Father". This designation of God as Father here is much more than a common phrase. It stands for the entire reality of God in his relation to the humankind and to the cosmos as a whole.

The Message of Matthew 5:48

The abiding message of the *mahavakya* in Matthew 5:48 is that it is the invitation of Jesus Christ which is extended to all to become more and more universal and cosmic in their thinking and living. In a pluralistic society like ours it is very important to be universal in our perception of realities and evaluation of issues. Ours is a pluralistic society and throughout the world there is a growing awareness of the need of accepting and respecting pluralism, although it brings in its train a series of issues and problems at the social, cultural, economic, political and religious levels. There are many immediate and mediate reasons behind the emergence of this pluralistic thinking, such as the progress of science and technology and the revolutionary influence of mass media. We have also to recognize the impact of philosophical and theological reflection characteristic of all religions in shaping and promoting such a pluralistic awareness. We also realize that we are living in a world characterized by profound and rapid change at all levels. It is universally experienced that the world has undergone more changes during the past fifty years than it witnessed during the preceding five hundred years. Our world is now characterized by a lot of mobility. There are mass movements of peoples going from one country to another in search of work or fleeing from war or other problems. Education has also become internationalized with students moving from one continent to the other. Tourism has opened up all five continents to people. As a result, religions also have opened their doors for all peoples. Never before has so much of information been available regarding the ways, in which different peoples of the world think, live and work. All these new developments create their own blessings and burdens. But all have to accept this new situation whether they like it or not.

World religions are also beginning to experience that their future and growth do not any more consist in isolation, but rather in their openness to other religions and their cultures. Those who are involved in religious discussions are also becoming more and more convinced that any attempt to dominate and monopolize in the realm of religion is self-defeating. There is no more question of any religious absolutes. It is more a question of sharing, learning from each other, enriching and being enriched. The time is gone for religions merely to sit together and discuss their dogmatic and ethical differences and come to some common agreement. The time is also gone for one religion to teach others about what is right and what is wrong. There is nothing much that can be achieved in having official documents published about the positive attitudes religions must have towards each other. What is more important and imperative is the role religions have to play in a pluralistic society of our times to guide it, to inspire it and also to challenge it. In other words, the pluralistic world of our times demands that what is of utmost importance is the coming together of the world religions for a common programme of action to make the world a better place for people to live and work.

More than anything that could take place at the level of inter-religious relationship, the real challenge facing religions in our pluralistic world is how these religions can come together to work for a more just and dignified society throughout the world. Beyond all intellectual discussions, this new approach to inter-religious relationship must prepare all religions to engage themselves in a common programme of social involvement for the emergence of a better human society. Religions have to be above politics of all kinds and so they can come together, plan and work together for a better world, and render a better deal to humanity. On the one hand, religions must stand together to face the manifold problems facing humanity with arise from technology, urbanization, industrialization, and, on the other hand, widespread poverty, population expansion, unemployment and the widening gap between the developed and developing nations. It is in this tragic situation affecting the whole humanity that religions as a whole have to be conscientized. They must be made to realize their important role to face these challenges and do something concrete and meaningful to save the humankind from this precarious situation.[11] What we need for this joint action and involvement is not only conviction and motivation, but also an emotional attachment to the cause they stand for. Ideologies and principles are in plenty, theoretical formulations there are many. But simple and inviting thoughts we do not evolve many which inspire humans and persuade them to action and involvement.

The Transreligious Challenge of Matthew 5:48

Through the *mahavakya* we have analysed above Jesus is placing before the world the ultimate and convincing reasons why all religions must work together for the emergence of a new society. It is all concerned about the basic reality of our human nature and existence on this earth as brothers and sisters, as children of the same God. Jesus did not invent this as a new idea, he only analysed it on the basis of the premises he saw around him. But it needed courage and optimism to formulate his ideas and also to stand for them. Hence Jesus of Nazareth had to face oppositions, confront criticism and undergo the tragic experience of dying on the cross. Jesus is not the founder of a religion in the technical sense of the word, although many would consider it that way. What he did was to evolve a new way of being and behaving, a new way of relating oneself to others, to God and also to other humans. To articulate this new teaching Jesus introduced the concepts of kingdom of God, the Fatherhood of God and universal brotherhood and sisterhood of all humans. What Jesus aimed at was the gradual emergence of a new society which transcends the barriers of caste, colour and creed. It is this universal outlook which Jesus gave expression to in the *mahavakya* about the perfection and maturity of God the Father which is proposed to all humans as something to be practised by them.

As we have tried to formulate in the beginning of this study, it is through words that such profound ideas are articulated and communicated. Word is the sublime articulation of the human and divine reality. It is through sublime words that humans communicate their innermost convictions and aspirations to others. Saints and sages, philosophers and theologians communicate their ideas to others through their spoken and written words. When it is the question of the divine word, it brings with it

---

[11] "Religions and the Ultimate Concerns of Man: India's Response" in *Critical and Creative* (Bangalore: Dharmaram Publications, 1986) pp. 172-179.

more power and persuasion. Religious scriptures of world religions have preserved a great collection of such divine words and they are a patrimony and heritage of the whole humankind. Now that religions are coming closer and are experiencing the benefits of being and working together, a study of the inspiring sayings of these religious scriptures will prove very encouraging and rewarding. What makes such studies and sharing of experience meaningful is our readiness to step out of the immediate circles of our religious identity and open our minds and hearts to appreciate the beauty of religious complementarity. Jesus tried to make the basis of his Gospel rest on universal principles and it is the duty of all who take his teaching seriously to focus their attention on issues that are universal and all-embracing. This is precisely what Mahatma Gandhi, the Father of the Indian Nation, did as part of his noble ideal and goal of *satyagraha*, his search and struggle for truth.

VII

GOD'S REIGN AND WORLD RELIGIONS

It is a very encouraging and consoling fact that in recent times Christianity has emerged as one of the most tolerant religions, and this tolerant attitude we can observe in many areas of secular and religious thinking, such as the attitude of the Church towards the world, secular ideologies, political systems as well as the new findings of technology and human sciences. Above all, this tolerance is visible in the positive attitude Christianity has developed towards other world religions, and this phenomenon is to be understood and appreciated against the background of its traditional negative attitude, its claim to uniqueness and universality and a consequent feeling of its superiority over all other religions. Though these claims are not altogether given up, there is a significant change of perspective visible in many areas of inter-religious relationship. The Roman Catholic Church and the World Council of Churches have both taken bold steps in their understanding and appreciation of other world religions. In the World Council of Churches the first inter-religious meeting was held in 1969 at Ajaltoun, Lebanon, and later in 1971 a separate sub-unit for "Dialogue with People of Living Faiths and Ideologies" was constituted. In the Roman Catholic Church a major breakthrough happened with the Vatican II Declaration on the Relationship of the Church to Non-Christian Religions[1] in 1965, known as *Nostra Aetate*. As Cardinal Bea, the chief architect of *Nostra Aetate*, observes, this Declaration should lead to effective action in various churches. Its principle and spirit should inspire the lives of all Christians, so that the spirit of dialogue already initiated by the Popes during the previous years may bear fruits in the future. It is doubtful whether the message contained in this prophetic statement of the Cardinal has been sufficiently accepted by many in the Roman Catholic Church. He continues: "It is in the fruits which this declaration should and will have after the Council that its main importance lies. The Declaration is an important and promising beginning, yet no more than the beginning of a long and demanding way towards the arduous goal of a humanity whose members feel themselves truly the sons (and daughters) of the same Father in heaven and act on this conviction".[2]

---

[1] It is unfortunate that the expression "Non-Christian Religions" is still being used by many Christians as something taken for granted. In fact, it is an expression which qualifies other religions only in terms of a negative aspect, whereas, as a matter of fact, all these religions have their own positive characteristics and values. It is high time to stop this expression also in the documents of the Church, an expression inherited from Western missionaries.

[2] A. Bea quoted from Fesquet, *Le Journal du Concile,* ed. By R. Morel, 1966, p. 120.

It is in the spirit of this new openness to other world religions that in 1986 Pope John Paul II initiated a day of prayer for peace at Assisi, to which he invited 50 Christians and 50 leaders of other religions, which was an act of dialogue in the highest degree. The implications of this event go far beyond the event itself. It confers a theological legitimacy, necessity and imperative for inter-religious dialogue, not only for the sake of various religions to come together and relate to each other, but also for the religions to become conscious of their task of bringing about peace at all levels in our contemporary society. Again, on February 5, 1986 Pope John Paul II during his historic visit to India addressed a gathering of about 300 representatives of world's great religions in Madras, India, such as Hinduism, Islam, Christianity, Sikhism, Jainism, Buddhism, Zoroastrianism and Judaism, and spoke to them about the importance of inter-religious dialogue for the welfare and progress of humanity. He also characterized India as the "cradle of religious traditions" and paid tribute to the spirit of tolerance and co-operation among religions that had always been part of the Indian heritage. In fact, India, which is the home of many important world religions, has contributed very much towards inter-religious dialogue and understanding as well as appreciation among religions throughout its history. The Pope was aware of this fact and his appreciation of the religious and philosophical traditions of India is clearly articulated in his recent Encyclical *Fides et Ratio*.[3]

The New Atmosphere of Inter-Religious Relationship

When we try to understand the reasons behind the emergence of this new climate of inter-religious relationship and mutual appreciation among religions promoted by the Church, it is not all clear as to what has prompted this new phenomenon. It is not at all correct to understand it as opportunism on the part of Church now to speak a language of condescension and magnanimity to make up for the sins of the past because Christianity had been a very intolerant religion during the past several centuries. Nor is it correct to maintain that this is a new tactic to win over other religions to the side of Christianity and thereby to convert them, as some still continue to remark. The real point is that there has been a radical re-thinking and re-appraisal on the part of various Churches on the reality of religions in God's plan of salvation, and this fact cannot be denied at all. It must be emphasized that several factors have worked together for the emergence of this new climate, among which the impact of a new world vision (*Weltanschauung*) holds an important place. Basic to this new world vision is the recognition of pluralism as a constituent dimension of this world, of human life and human activities as a whole. More than ever before, humankind is becoming more and more aware of its being in a pluralistic world. In fact, pluralism is the basic datum of contemporary thinking and living all over the world. Pluralism means the acceptance of the

---

[3] *Fides et Ratio* art. 72.

other as the *other* with all its uniqueness, not as something opposed to oneself nor as an extension of oneself, but as something with its own inalienable qualities and characteristics. Pluralism also denotes the concept of the one and the many, the one as something basic to all things, coordinating the many and the many as coordinated to the one, thereby creating harmony and peace among the many. Once pluralism is accepted as a basic reality of this world and its historical process at all levels, it becomes easier for all to see the legitimacy of the other to exist and to operate at various levels of life and the positive role pluralism plays in enriching all. It is this richness of pluralism that reveals the beauty of our human community as a whole, because God has created a world characterized by its own basic pluralism at various levels, both biological and non-biological. Religious pluralism is seen by many as an articulation of this basic pluralism characteristic of our human community and of the world at large.

Besides this pluralistic thinking, we also realize that we are living in a world characterized by profound and rapid changes at all levels. It is universally experienced that the world has undergone more changes during the past fifty years than it witnessed during the preceding five hundred years and more. Our world is characterized by a lot of mobility. In fact, mobility is part and parcel of life. Long ago Heraclitus (ca 500 BCE) wrote: "Everything flows". Everything is in a state of movement. We cannot step into the same river twice because the water that is the river is flowing. World Religions are also beginning to experience that their progress and growth do not any more consist in their isolated existence, but rather in openness to other religions and to the cultures of other peoples and thereby joining this process of change and growth. Those who are involved in religious affairs are also becoming more and more convinced that any attempt on their part to dominate or monopolize in the realm of religion is self-defeating. There is no more question of religious or cultural absolutes. Equally excluded is the tendency to establish one's own religion or culture as something normative for the whole humankind. As a matter of fact, this pluralistic and dynamic thinking in the understanding of religion is one of the most crucial issues affecting contemporary discussions on religion, especially in the context of the emergence of new religious movements and practices. Religious pluralism also deeply affects the Church's self-understanding and her mission in the world. Traditionally known as a Christian country, Europe is now realizing that there Christians have to live together with the followers of other religions, millions of whom are now living in those countries. In the Asian countries the situation is very different. There the Christians have been living and working in the midst of other religions for thousands of years. All these phenomena necessitate a great deal of re-thinking and re-appraisal on the part of the Christians who have been so far trained for a monolithic understanding of their religion during the past several centuries and now it is a demanding task for them. But they have to face this challenge and must develop a new approach as part of their mission in the world.

Coming to the specific question of the intolerant and negative attitude of Christianity towards other religions during the past, it is to be stated that an unscientific and uncritical interpretation and understanding of the Bible has also played a big role in the approach of the Christians towards other religions. Biblical exegetes did not pay sufficient attention to the fact that the Bible is the Word of God in human language and that the human dimension of the Bible accounts for many of the negative statements in it about the followers of other religions. So it has been customary in the past for Christian theologians and exegetes to have recourse to the Old and New Testament as advocating a negative attitude towards other religions. During the colonial periods missionaries from the West used this method as part of their efforts to convert the followers of other religions to Christianity. The Church histories of this period contain many references to the followers of other religions as 'worshippers of the devil'. In CE 1540 the temples of Hinduism in the islands of Goa were destroyed in accordance with the consent of the king of Portugal, and the celebration of Hindu rites and feasts were banned. The so-called holy wars waged by Israel against the nations surrounding them and their gods, the condemnation of the nations by the prophets, the strong criticism of idolatry in some books of the Old Testament,[4] the hatred and antipathy practiced by the post-exilic Judaism towards the Gentiles, all helped the Church, her missionaries and her theologians to continue the same negative attitude towards other religions, including Judaism.

Moreover, the New Testament also gives us indications about how some of its writers, such as Paul, speak about the Gentiles as "offering sacrifices to demons and not to God" (1 Cor 10:20-21), or brand the entire Gentile world as given up to idolatry and immorality (Rom 1:18-32). The critical and negative remarks Paul makes about the incongruity of any relationship between Christian faith and Gentile religions in 2 Cor 6:14-7:1 is sufficient proof of how the early Christians were taught to keep away from any contact with other religions.[5] The same attitude continued till very recent times. From the New Testament passages were culled to substantiate a thesis that Jesus rejected many others from his vision about the future of his ministry. Thus on the basis of Mt 10:5 Jesus was presented as one who prohibited his disciples to go the Samaritans and Gentiles. Mt 15:26 was cited as Jesus referring to the Gentiles as 'dogs'. If we closely follow the dynamics of this story, it becomes clear that it is to praise the faith of the Canaanite woman that

---

[4] Cf. Is 2:6-22; Bar 6:1-72; Wis 13:1-14:31

[5] The authenticity of this passage is doubtful, especially because the passage obstructs the flow of thought between 6:11-13 and 7:2-4. In any case, the passage is out of context. It is possible that it is a later interpolation, especially because here we have the only reference in the Bible to the principle of evil as Belial, an expression current in the Qumran writings.

this reference is made by Jesus, a customary reference used by the Jews about the Gentiles. Since the Bible was explained and understood exclusively as the Word of God, no attention was paid to its being also the human word which fact brought in many of the limitations of its various authors, such as historical, cultural, psychological and religious. Added to that, when Paul was being persecuted by the Jews of Northern Greece, he himself characterized his parent religion of Judaism as one "displeasing to God and hostile to all humankind, filling up their quota of sins and bringing down the wrath of God upon it" (1 Thes 2:14-16). There is no wonder then that the teaching derived from such passages amounted to a totally negative and depreciatory attitude of Christianity towards other religions during the past many centuries. This could very well be seen in some of the prayers of the Roman Catholic Church before Vatican II.[6]

Together with these exaggerations in the understanding of biblical texts, there arose also a wrong understanding of mission based on the longer ending of Mark (Mk 16:9-20) which insists on the need of faith and baptism as necessary for salvation: "The one who believes and is baptized will be saved; but the one who does not believe will be condemned" (Mk 16:16). This directive as an authentic teaching of Jesus prompted the missionaries to convert the followers of other religions in large numbers and to baptize them at all costs. So also the great commission in Mt 28:16-20 was interpreted as authorizing the Church to make disciples of all nations, baptizing them and enforcing on them the teaching of Jesus as necessary for their salvation.[7] Mission was understood as a spiritual conquest and it was exclusively conversion-oriented. Moreover, the major accent of mission was on the planting of the Church. In this method of interpreting biblical passages and applying them in missionary propaganda a very important principle of biblical hermeneutics was forgotten, namely, the need of a healthy balancing of diachronic and synchronic approach, namely, the balancing of the *then* of the biblical text characterized by its historical, geographical, cultural and psychological limitations with the *now* of the same biblical text which is to be interpreted and applied in the new sociological, cultural and psychological contexts of the contemporary society. The Bible is the Word of God in human language entrusted to the Church and her theologians, who have to respect both these dimensions as well as their specific historical, social, religious and cultural contexts.

---

[6] In a certain sense anti-Semitism seems to have its origin from this passage. During the Good Friday services there was a "prayer against the Jews" which after 1958 Pope John XXIII directed to be removed from the liturgical texts.

[7] Cf. Joseph Pathrapankal, "Bible and Missiological Challenges" in Paul Vadakumpadan, Mathew Kariapuram and Joseph Puthenpurackal (Ed), *Breaking New Ground in Mission* (Shillong: Vendrame Institute Publications, 2002) pp.219-246.

Scientific Study of the Bible and World Religions

But in recent times a radical change has taken place in the understanding of biblical texts and this has helped very much in the application of these biblical texts in relation to world religions, precisely because of the acceptance and application of a critical and scientific understanding of the Bible towards the end of the nineteenth century of the Common Era. In fact, it has been clearly established that the Word of God in the Bible is formulated in human language and the latter aspect is very much conditioned by the time, culture and psychology of the human authors of the Bible. Consequently, an objective study of any specific issue related to the Bible demands that we develop a critical and scientific approach to that subject and remain committed to it and then apply its conclusion to contemporary situations. It is true that in the Catholic Church it took more time for the official acceptance of the scientific method in biblical studies. It was in 1943 that Pope Pius XII not only accepted the principle of scientific studies but also maintained that scientific of the Bible is absolutely necessary. Vatican II strongly endorsed this approach and the present atmosphere in the Catholic Church is one of encouragement for the scientific study of the Bible. The latest document about the scientific study of the Bible is *The Interpretation of the Bible in the Church* promulgated in 1993.[8]

Moreover, it is also becoming clear to every unbiased reader of the Bible that both in the Old Testament and in the New Testament there are several issues discussed which show that both Israel and the early Church were ready to appreciate their neighbouring religions and their convictions and practices. Thus in the Old Testament we see many allusions to mythological concepts prevalent among other religions and literary forms borrowed from among the Mesopotamians. It was not a question of total rejection of these literary forms, but of a re-conception and re-formulation of prevailing concepts among these peoples. This basic openness to other religions and religious literature enabled the Old Testament writers to borrow names of God used among the Canaanites, such as *El Elyon* and *Baal Berit* and also to become inculturated to the Canaanite shrines of worship, such as Beersheba and Shechem. The well-known feasts of the Unleavened Bread, Pentecost and Tabernacles, celebrated by Israel after their settlement in Canaan (Ex 23:14-17), were originally harvest festivals which were borrowed from the Canaanites, but they were given new theological meanings in the context of Israel's saving history. The Jerusalem Temple built by Solomon was designed by Phoenician architects and it represented the adaptation of Canaanite culture right into the centre of Israel's life and worship. The sea in the Temple, which was supported by twelve bulls (1 Kgs 7:23-25), reflected the fertility and mythological motifs of the Fertile Crescent. The Temple was intended to be a

---

[8] Libreria Editrice Vaticana 1993.

replica of Yahweh's heavenly abode, a microcosm of the macrocosm, in line with the ancient view that there is a correspondence between the earthly and heavenly spheres.

When intolerance and antipathy towards other religions developed in the post-exilic Judaism which was headed by priestly leadership, especially by Ezra and Nehemiah, we once again see the bold steps taken up by some critical leaders, such as the authors of the books of Ruth and Jonah. At a time when Ezra and Nehemiah were strictly prohibiting inter-religious marriage on the basis of the Deuteronomistic law (Dt 7:1-6; Neh 13:23-27), the author of the book of Ruth posed a challenge through the story of a Moabite woman, Ruth. The story tells us how Ruth was providentially led from her Gentile home country to Bethlehem of Judea, where she married an influential citizen, Boaz, and became the great grandmother of David, Israel's greatest king. Many scholars believe that the story is a subtle piece of propaganda against the view that one's position within Israel was dependent upon purity of blood or correctness of genealogy, and it is a powerful and critical demonstration of how a Gentile woman can be a beneficial element for the community of Jews. Another critical writer of the post-exilic period is the author of the book of Jonah who presents his message in the guise of a story concerning a prophet who is presented as having lived back in the days of Jeroboam II (2 Kgs 14:25). This *haggada* is meant for driving home to the readers of the writer's generation a prophetic message that Yahweh's sovereignty is not circumscribed by the boundaries of the chosen community of Israel. He shows his mercy and love upon whom he will (Ex 33:19) and reveals his salvation in the most unexpected places. So the author rebukes the Jews for supposing in their pride that Yahweh's purpose was restricted to the preservation of the Jewish community, even at the cost of the destruction of the enemies of the Jews, and they are reminded that other people, supposedly rejected by God, are embraced within Yahweh's mercy and love.

It is against the background of this universal and pluralistic thinking on religion and its relationship with other religions found throughout the Old Testament that we have to look at the ministry and message of Jesus of Nazareth, who also came as a critical prophet of contemporary Judaism in order to reveal through his words and deeds his God-given commission of inaugurating a new religious movement, not at all circumscribed by the narrow ethnic and racial considerations of Judaism. In this Jesus of Nazareth followed the critical role played by the authors of the books of Ruth and Jonah because he was born of the line of Ruth (Mt 1:5) and he was himself someone greater than Jonah (Lk 11:32). Jesus of Nazareth came on the threshold of history with a specific message about God and humankind. It is to be emphasized that Jesus of Nazareth is not the founder of a religion in the ordinary sense of the word. He inaugurated a new religious movement and a corresponding life style and world vision, to promote which he had to carve out a new group of committed followers from the very religious reality, of which he and they were members in every aspect of membership in a religion. It is true that at a later stage in the context of the growth and articulation of this movement, as recorded in the Acts of the Apostles, there was a tendency among some leaders of the Jerusalem Christian community to consider it more as a sect, and the adverse effects of this myopic vision were there for several decades down through the first century of the Common Era.

As part of his new understanding of religion, Jesus invited all to a radical *metanoia*, irrespective of whether they were Jews or Gentiles. In a certain sense Jesus was a marginal Jew,[9] understanding this marginality as a transcendent dimension of his personality. He associated himself with all, Jews, Samaritans and Gentiles, rich and poor, holy people and sinners, even to the extent of being criticized by the leaders of the Jewish community (Lk 15:2). Through these critical actions Jesus wanted to evolve a new community which transcended all religions and their structural limitations. It may be observed here that during the early centuries of Christian preaching there was not the slightest idea that by accepting the message of Christ one was changing over from one religion to another; rather it was a question of a new loyalty, a new conviction and a new commitment to Christ. What Jesus did was to show the new way that leads to a new life. He even emphasized the need of a non-localized religion and a transcendent form of worship in so far as God is spirit and those who worship him must worship him in spirit and truth (Jn 4:23). It is important to note that this whole discussion on religion and worship between Jesus and the Samaritan woman took place in Samaria, far away from Jerusalem, the official seat of Jewish religion, which thought that it had the full right to interpret the meaning and nature of religion for the whole humankind.

In the light of these considerations we have to evaluate the inner meaning of some narratives in the Gospels where we see Jesus transcending the boundaries of his own religion and appreciating the Gentiles and the Samaritans for their profound religiosity. Seeing the profound faith of a Roman officer of Capernaum, who went to Jesus with a request to cure his servant who was ill, Jesus told those who followed him: "Truly, I say to you, not even in Israel have I found such faith. I tell you, many will come from east and west and sit at table with Abraham, Isaac and Jacob in the kingdom of heaven, while the children of the kingdom will be thrown into the outer darkness" (Mt 8:10-12). To the Canaanite woman who showed her unfailing faith and trust in his saving power Jesus said: " O woman, great is your faith! Be it done for you as you desire" (Mt 15:28). The attitude of Jesus towards the Samaritans is yet another clear proof to show how keen Jesus was to bring together communities of opposing loyalties with his courageous traveling

---

[9] Cf. John P. Meier, *A Marginal Jew* (New York: Doubleday, Vol. I 1991; Vol. II 1994.

through the region of Samaria, much against the conventions of his parent religion (Jn 4:4-42). Through his encounter with the Samaritan woman Jesus brought the whole community of the Samaritans to a very friendly relationship. There was no dispute or discussion on orthodoxy or orthopraxis between Jesus and the Samaritans. In the parable on "Who is the neighbour?" it is a Samaritan and not a Jew who is presented by Jesus as the ideal neighbour (Lk 10:25-37). As a member of Judaism it should have been very difficult for Jesus to speak in this manner, but as one who had the capacity to transcend the externals, human conventions and ethnic considerations, he praised the Samaritan for his readiness to become the neighbour, and presented him as an example to be followed: "Go and do likewise" (Lk10:37), Jesus told the lawyer. The same truth is once again affirmed in the story of the ten lepers. The one who came back to thank Jesus for the gift of healing he had received was a Samaritan. Jesus' reaction to this extraordinary gesture is noteworthy: "Were not ten cleansed? Where are the nine? Was no one found to return and give praise to God except this foreigner?" (Lk 17:17-18). These stories and parables bring out very clearly the fact that for Jesus religion and faith were not the exclusive privilege of the Jews, and that there must be a dimension of religion through which all have to reach out to the others and appreciate them for their inner goodness and generosity.

The story of the Greeks who went to Jerusalem to worship and who wanted to meet Jesus is one of the most challenging stories in the Gospel of John, which shows how Jesus understood his own religious identity and his relation to the followers of other religions (Jn 12:20-26). It is a story about some devout Gentiles, who may have been preparing themselves to become followers of Judaism, in which connection they had gone to Jerusalem for the celebration of a feast. There in Jerusalem, these Gentiles were impressed by the person and message of Jesus, who was basically a Jew for them. Narrated as an event towards the end of the Book of Signs (Jn 1-12) in John, this story is to be seen also as a semiotic narrative with an abiding message for the followers of all religions.[10] It provides for them some profound insights in the form of openness and appreciation that should be characteristic of the followers of all religions. The message of this story consists in how Jesus reacted to the concept of religious identity as understood by the two disciples of Jesus, Philip and Andrew, who must have thought that Jesus would have his own reservations about meeting with those Gentiles for the simple reason that he was a Jew. The reaction of Jesus to this wrong impression of the disciples is spelt out in the reference to the glory Jesus was looking forward to, namely, the moment of his passion and death when he would at last cease to be a Jew and would be lifted up above all considerations of creed and caste (Jn 12:32).

---

[10] Cf. Joseph Pathrapankal, "Jesus and the Greeks: Reflections on a Theology of Religious Identity" in *Critical and Creative: Studies in Bible and Theology* (Bangalore: Dharmaram Publications, 1986) pp. 71-84.

Thereby Jesus was referring to the event of his transcending the barriers and limitations of his own human and religious conditions of being a Jew. His mission was something far surpassing his Jewish identity. What he wanted was to make all humans rise above the limiting factors of their religious identity and build up a new humanity and a new society.

A very bold presentation of openness in religious thinking in the New Testament is found in the letter to the Hebrews, where the author presents the person of Jesus Christ to his readers as someone whom they should follow at all costs, showing them how he was the priestly mediator for them in their struggle for a meaningful Christian life. As they were about to give up their newly accepted Christian faith in favour of their old faith and its practices, the author explains to them the grandeur of the Christian call which is centred on the person of Christ, who was a better and greater priest than the priests of the Old Covenant. Then the author explains this priesthood of Christ taking the model from a priest of the Jebusites, known as Melchizedek (Gen 14:17-24). The author did not have any scruple at all to take such a model from another religion to present his theology of the priesthood of Christ because for him the important thing was how best this Jebusite priest realized in himself the ideals of a good mediator between God and humans. These ideals he could not see in the priesthood of the Old Covenant which was characterized by externalism and legalism, and so he turned to a model from another religion (Heb 7:1-28).

The above analysis about the importance of a scientific study of the Old and New Testaments, which reveals many areas of positive and tolerant attitude towards other religions, invites us to engage in the search for a new paradigm within which we have to situate these new orientations. This is particularly true of what we have seen about the challenging ministry of Jesus. How could Jesus carry out his mission with his consistent emphasis on universal and transcendent principles in all what he said and did? Was it question of some kind of opportunism through which Jesus wanted to impress upon people and canvass them for broadening the dimensions of his religious movement? Can we still find some foundational thought pattern that controls the universal and all-embracing orientations we discover in the teaching and actions of Jesus? Can we arrive at a biblical concept which we can maintain as the controlling thought which encourages and legitimizes these universal and transcendent dimensions of the biblical religion towards other religions? It seems that we do have such an all-embracing idea in the concept of the kingdom of God which is basic to the biblical religion and around which Jesus understood his ministry and presented his preaching and teaching. In fact, the concept of the kingdom of God encompasses within itself the principles and parameters of a religious outlook which can coordinate and enhance such a pluralisitic and universal approach. Since the expression 'kingdom of God' carries with it a static and geographical nuance, it has become customary among theologians and exegetes to render this concept through a more dynamic expression, namely, *God's Reign*, meaning thereby the active guidance and providence of God extended to the entire humankind and the cosmic order. It is a concept that embraces the totality of human life far above all religious considerations, and it has a reference to the entire humankind its historical process, past, present and future.

God's Reign and its Universal Perspectives

The importance of the concept of the kingdom of God in the preaching and teaching of Jesus is clear to anyone studying the Synoptic Gospels. The expression 'kingdom of God' occurs 13 times in Mark, 31 times in Luke and 33 times in Matthew, mostly as 'kingdom of heaven',[11] twice in John, corresponding to the Hebrew *malekuth* and the Aramaic *malekutha* and the Greek *basileia*. Here the concept of the kingdom is not to be understood spatially, but operationally. It is God's sovereign activity over the whole cosmos. It means a quality of existence and a state of being in which God exercises his providential care over all. It is a concept derived from the Old Testament acclamation: "Yahweh rules as king" (*Yahweh malak*) and the prophetic promise: "Yahweh will reign as king" (*Yahweh yimlok*), a concept related to creation, deliverance and the constant care of the people by Yahweh. In fact, the concept of the kingdom is more a deep symbol, which Norman Perrin calls a 'tensive symbol', which evokes a whole range of meanings, and so it cannot be properly defined. It does not have just one meaning but a whole range of meanings. It is not correct to try to reduce it to any one idea or conception,[12] because it is a multifaceted reality. It is more a story than a concept that can be neatly described in words and concepts. It tells a story, starting from the creation of this good and ordered universe, the corruption of the creation through human sin, God's gracious choice of the people of Israel, their liberation from Egypt through the power of Yahweh, their experience of salvation at mount Sinai, their desert journey and their entrance into the promised land. It is also related to the institution of human kingship in Israel, with its ideal king in David, God's choice of Jerusalem and mount Zion for his dwelling place, the disasters caused by David's less than ideal successors, the descent of Israel into ever greater idolatry and sin, Israel's rejection of the prophets' warning, the destruction of the northern kingdom and later that of Jerusalem and the consequent Babylonian captivity, the promise of a future restoration that would include a rebuilt Jerusalem and a new purified Temple and the final establishment among humans of God's eternal kingdom of peace and justice.

---

[11] Matthew, following the custom of many rabbis, uses "kingdom of heaven" more often. Only four times (12:28; 19:24; 21:31,43) he uses 'kingdom of God'. The use of 'heaven' in place of 'God' is a pious Jewish periphrasis to avoid constantly naming God who is above all.

[12] Cf. N. Perrin, *Jesus and the Language of the Kingdom* (Philadelphia: Fortress Press, 1976).

This broad outline of Israel's history is the framework within which we have to situate the concept of the kingdom of God in the preaching and teaching of Jesus. The precise phrase 'kingdom of God' appears only very late in the Old Testament and remains relatively rare in the material written before or around the time of Jesus. But the central idea, as we have summarized above, remains basic to all historical happenings, and a concrete expression of the hope related to God's ultimate victory over all human endeavours and failures is basic to the concept of the kingdom of God. Jesus consciously decided to make this symbol of God's kingdom the central theme of his message. He seized upon this concept, the imagery and the language that was present, but hardly central to the Old Testament and inter-testamental traditions of Judaism and consciously and pointedly made the symbol of God's kingly rule the central part of his message, his words as well as deeds. He understood this concept in terms of the definitive coming of God into this world to bring the present state of things to an end and to establish his full and unimpeded guidance over the world. While this symbol continued to be used during the inter-testamental period to refer to God's kingship in Israel's past and present as well as throughout eternity, the symbol was especially prominent in eschatological and apocalyptic context. Often there were also political overtones associated with this concept. But Jesus de-emphasized the apocalyptic overtones associated with the kingdom and removed its political bias. Although the urgent tone of Jesus' message emphasized the imminence of the kingdom's arrival, Jesus, unlike much of apocalyptic literature, did not set any timetable for the kingdom's eschatological appearance.

There is a central question that is being discussed about how Jesus understood the eschatological and existential nature of this kingdom. In the past there had been a rich variety of opinions and theories. The best approach to this question seems to be to understand this issue within the context of the thought-patterns of the early Church and not in terms of our contemporary reckoning of time where we go by dates, months and year as in a calendar. So theories such as consistent eschatology and realized eschatology have nothing to contribute towards a realistic understanding of what Jesus meant by the coming of the kingdom of God. For Jesus, the kingdom of God was at the same time a present and a future reality. Thus we pray for the coming of the kingdom (Mt 6:10), Jesus speaks about drinking wine in the kingdom of God as a future event (Mk 14:25) and there are indications in several sayings of Jesus that the kingdom has eschatological overtones. The fullness of salvation wrought by God in Christ transcends this world and the kingdom of God in the preaching of Jesus also has this eschatological aspect. At the same time, Jesus also refers to the reality of the kingdom as something present. In his first proclamation Jesus referred to the kingdom of God as something near (Mk 1:14-15). He told the disciples of John the Baptist that the kingdom with its liberating presence was active among them (Mt 11:2-6). In the Beelzebul controversy Jesus refers to the active presence of the kingdom of God as opposed to the kingdom of Satan, together with a statement about his driving out the demons through the finger of God, finger understood as a point of reference to the power of God (Mt 12:28). The clearest teaching of Jesus about the presence of the kingdom of God we have in Lk 17:20-21. When the Pharisees asked Jesus when the kingdom of God was coming, Jesus answered them with a negative statement that it does not come through sensational events and then he told them that the kingdom of God is among them, meaning thereby that it was operating among the people.[13]

It seems that more important than the eschatological and existential aspects of the kingdom is how Jesus dwelt on the central message of the kingdom as something characterized by the providential care of God as the Father of the entire humankind and the whole cosmic order. What is important for us to see is how Jesus brings in through the concept of the Fatherhood of God a personal dimension to the whole concept of the kingdom of God. Whether we use the expression 'kingdom of God' or 'Reign of God' or 'Rule of God' matters little, if we are not giving sufficient attention to the inner dynamics of this new state of affairs, this new quality of existence. Nowhere does Jesus speak about God as the king. God is always the Father, the *abba*. He cares for all his children and he wants them to have full trust and confidence in him. It is this picture of the Father[14] that Jesus tries to emphasize throughout the Sermon on the Mount. It is from this concept of God as the Father of the entire cosmos that all relations take on a new meaning and a new dynamism, which transcend caste, colour and creed. For Jesus God is the Father, all are God's children and among them all are brothers and sisters. This universalism is basic and central to Jesus' teaching about the kingdom of God and it is also the major matrix within which we have to understand the uniqueness of his teaching. It seems that Jesus took over this concept of the kingdom, which was otherwise not so important in the Old Testament and in inter-testamental literature as well as in the writings of Qumran, precisely to charge and fill it with these important ideas about the personal dimensions of the new situation he came to establish here on earth.

---

[13] For more details about the future and present aspects of the kingdom of God in the teaching of Jesus see John P. Meier, *A Marginal Jew* vol. II (New York: Doubleday, 1994) pp. 289-506.

[14] Through this expression there is no attempt made to continue the Patriarchal language of our traditional theology. In the absence of a better word we still have to use the conventional one trying to see in it the aspects of Father and Mother. The attempt to introduce 'Parent' as an inclusive concept may not evoke sufficient personal touch.

God's Reign and the New Humanity in the Vision of Jesus

More important for us to understand is how Jesus tried to establish God's Reign among the people as a concrete reality affecting the life of the people as a whole. On the one hand, he tried to reach out to all humans without exception, and this was an expression of his understanding of the God's Reign as extending to all. Since God is the *abba* of the entire humankind, he is concerned about all and Jesus also revealed this universalism in all what he said and did. But this universalism does not mean anything unless there is a corresponding style of action through which the meaning of this universalism is manifested and realized. In other words, God's Reign can become a reality only to the extent of the blessings of God's kingdom made available to humans. To be included in the realm of God's Reign should mean that humans are empowered to live in a manner befitting their human dignity as the children of God. This is precisely what Jesus was doing through his many saving actions, such as healing the sick, feeding the hungry and casting out the demons from those who were suffering from the oppression of the evil. Corresponding to his positive and universal attitude to the followers of all religions, Jesus was also extending his saving activity to all, namely, Jews, Gentiles and Samaritans. The marginalized and the neglected in the society were the primary beneficiaries of his saving actions. Jesus wanted to establish the foundations of a new humanity that is governed by higher and noble principles derived the concept of God's kingdom.

The Synoptic Gospels narrate that Jesus started his ministry in Galilee after John was arrested. We know from the Gospel of Mark that John was arrested as part of a political conspiracy (Mk 6:14-29) and it also constituted the backdrop of Jesus announcing the kingdom of God and inviting people to be converted and believe in the good news of the kingdom of God. Galilee was the homeland of economically and religiously backward people of Palestine.[15] It was also known as the Galilee of the Gentiles (Mt 4:15). The inner meaning of conversion and faith which Jesus emphasized was not only a spiritual preparation; rather it meant the challenge of accepting new values and new attitudes to life and to persons. Palestine during the time of Jesus was a country known for its political, racial, religious and economic oppression. It is in the context of these oppressive structures that Jesus gave his message, taught the people, performed miracles and cast out demons. In so far as the kingdom of God was a present reality moving towards its eschatological realization, Jesus wanted also a larger society that would correspond to the inner nature of this divine offer and imperative. The main source of Jesus

---

[15] Cf. George M. Soares-Prabhu "The Kingdom of God: Jesus' Vision of a New Society" in D.S. Amalorpavadass (ed) *The Indian Church in the Struggle for a New Society*" (Bangalore:NBCLC, 1981) pp. 579-607.

advocating the cause for this new society was his own *abba*-experience which gave him the framework within which he spelt out the qualities and characteristics of his disciples and all those who followed him. In the same way as Yahweh, the God of Israel, was one who acts[16] in human history, standing on the side of the poor and the oppressed, so also the *abba* of the Kingdom of God is one who is on the side of the marginalized and the poor, and Jesus made it a point to be on their side to defend them and protect them. The major difference is that God, the Father, does things in a more personal and gentle manner with his fatherly and motherly concerns. Jesus was the embodiment of these concerns and the Gospels describe how he was committed to his cause in the context of a series of opposition from the Jewish authorities. For Jesus, the kingdom of God was a critical reality and to be committed to the kingdom of God was to take a stance towards a critical role.

When we speak about Jesus envisaging a new society, we do not mean that he gave a blueprint of such a society which we can easily put into practice in our times. What we mean is that there are suggestive and indicative concepts in the teaching of Jesus which we have to translate into praxis. This is precisely the task of theologians and exegetes. The Bible as the Word of God committed to writing in human words is now entrusted to the Church and her theologians to critically study and apply to their situations in the concrete contexts of their theological activity. It is wrong to think that only clearly formulated concepts in the Bible can be applied to our times. The Bible is the Word of God, it is also the author's word as well as the interpreter's word. The interpretation has to remain faithful to the Word of God and also to the human author, but it should also respond to the needs and aspirations of the people who are living today. Theologians and exegetes must work together to understand the problems facing the human society in our times as a result of the great mistakes committed against powerless countries and their people by the mighty and the powerful.[17]

Jesus' vision of the new society was one that was part of the inaugurated eschatology, which would grow into bigger dimensions and proportions through the work of his disciples. It was to be a community characterized by inner freedom, love, fellowship and peace. It has to foster universalism, freedom and friendship and promote justice. It has to be a referent of historical liberation wherever it is called for. Jesus is on the side of the poor, but not on the side of poverty. The important point is that the poor

---

[16] Although several meanings have been given to the divine name YHWH in Ex 3:14, the most acceptable seems to be "He who causes to be what comes into existence", especially by W. F. Albright.

[17] Cf. .J.Pathrapankal, "Interpretation of the Word: God's Word, the Human Word and the Interpreter's Word" in *Text and Context* (Bangalore: *Dharma*ram Publications, 1993) pp. 1-16.

and the marginalized are pre-disposed to accept the message of the kingdom because of their trust in God and not in themselves. It is a society consisting of this category of people Jesus was gradually building up in the company of his chosen disciples who were to become pioneers of liberation and freedom for all humans and for the whole world. The sign events through which Jesus established the contours of this new society, such as his healing the sick, feeding the hungry, stilling the storm and raising the dead back to life should constitute the paradigms for his disciples to act, through which they should also build up communities all over the world where people can live in freedom and peace, enjoying their earthly life as something meaningful and at the same time moving towards its eschatological fulfillment.

God's Reign and World Religions through History

The Pastoral Constitution on the Church in the Modern World has given some very important insights about the new society and the kingdom of God as envisaged by Jesus: "While we are warned that it profits a man nothing if he gain the whole and lose himself ((Lk 9:25), the expectation of a new earth must not weaken but rather stimulate our concern for cultivating this one. For here grows the body of a new human family, a body which even now is able to give some kind of foreshadowing of the new age. Earthly progress must be carefully distinguished from the growth of Christ's kingdom. Nevertheless, to the extent that the former can contribute to the better ordering of human society, it is of vital concern to the kingdom of God".[18] These optimistic notes, in spite of their vagueness, go a long way in creating and cherishing hope in the hearts of men and women who want to see a better meaning for their earthly pilgrimage. What is basic to this vision of a new society is the positive and humanistic approach the teaching of the Church is now developing in her several documents which encourage her children to get involved in this secular city of theirs to make it a better place for the children of God to live in.

It is in the context of this vision of Jesus about a new human community as related to God's reign that we have to see the new style of relationship we have to build up between religions. In this approach Christians, supported and encouraged by the universal insights spread throughout the Bible, especially in the words and deeds of Jesus, have to take a lead and courageously build bridges of cooperation and destroy the barriers created through the centuries. The reality of religious pluralism demands on the part of the Church and her missionaries and the evangelizers a great respect for the traditions and practices of other religions, already recognized in *Nostra Aetate* and similar documents of the WCC. Christians have to move beyond the

---

[18] *GS* art. 39.

concept of dialogue of ideas towards a dialogue of life and a dialogue of action. The fear that it would encourage a kind of religious syncretism and a diluting of the message of the gospel is something that comes more from a superiority complex and lack of concern for others.

Secondly, the new culture of inter-religious relationship will remain a myth and a sophisticated idea as well as an intellectual recreation unless it prepares all religions to engage themselves in a common programme of social involvement for the creation of a better human society. Religions must stand together to face the manifold problems of humanity, which are arising from technology, urbanization, industrialization, on the one hand, and widespread poverty, population expansion, unemployment and the widening gap between the developed and developing nations, on the other hand. There is so much of exploitation, oppression and discrimination on the basis of caste, colour and creed practised all over the world. It calls for the application of some basic values of the kingdom of God which are ignored not only by political systems but also by religious traditions in general. Religions must stand together to face these problems. More than ever before, the world is facing the paradox of great affluence in certain sections of the world and of the society, on the one side, and on the other side, the vast majority of humanity, which had its expectations raised by the progress in science and technology, suffering from a great deal of poverty and deprivation of the basic amenities of life. The gap between the affluent countries and the so-called developing nations keeps on widening. Some western sociologists and economists have already written off the millions of the poor nations of the world as beyond redemption and have described all efforts to save them as a colossal waste of the meagre resources available. In fact, it would appear that in our present context of diminishing natural resources, the poor nations have to be kept poor if the rich have to continue to be rich and maintain their paradoxical standard of living.

Religions, which are supposed to be above politics, can and have to plan and work together for a better world, and for this they have to fight against all forms of exploitation whether at the national or international levels. The ultimate goal of all these efforts is to create a new society in which humans can live in dignity, harmony and healthy relationship. God created the humankind as one big family; religions are expected to maintain this holy heritage and build up this family and make it more and more united and integrated. To come to this understanding of mission and evangelization the Churches have to undergo a process of *tapas* and engage themselves in a *satyagraha*, a process in which they have to suffer along with the followers of other religions and also with the poor and the oppressed. It is this *tapas* and *satyagraha* which Jesus performed to inaugurate a new way of life in the context of the new situation of the kingdom of God he preached. The earlier this is taken care of, the better it is for the world. Jesus promised the Spirit to the disciples to assist them in their ministry and he said: "When the Spirit of truth comes, he will guide you into the whole truth (*pasa aletheia*) (Jn 16:13). The whole truth is not with us, it is with God and we are all marching towards that truth, seeking and finding, but always aware of the fact that we see it as in a mirror, dimly, and knowing only in part (1 Cor 13:12). Here it is a question of theological prudence and Christian humility not to identify the part with the whole and the shade with the reality.

The new climate of inter-religious relationship which we have tried to articulate calls for a new world vision and a new style of inter-religious relationship and operation. First of all, it demands that the followers of religions are to be characterized at the same time by religious authenticity, on the one hand, and a religious complementary approach, on the other hand. This can be achieved only from their readiness to accept their religion as the immediate context of their religious experience and at the same time open themselves to the other religions to be complemented by the religious experience of their fellow-humans. It is a realm in which all religions, keeping their own identity, should become authentic and open, and at the same time strive to reach beyond their own limited horizons of vision in relation to God, humanity and the world. We have to understand this process as an ongoing one in which all religions have to engage themselves in all humility and courage, with dedication and determination. It is no betrayal of one's own religious commitment, nor is it an acceptance of religious indifferentism. If God is the ultimate goal and end of all religions, he can be reached only through this process of transcendence, and all religions have to undergo a painful process of *kenosis* and transformation to arrive at this goal.

The concept of the kingdom of God and God's providential care over history gives the new rationale of openness to other religions beyond the present climate of inter-religious relationship practised in our times. This concept gives a new impetus and new vigour to consider the pluralistic structure of the world and of humanity from a new perspective of personalism and universalism. With its personalistic and universal parameters the Bible invites us to broaden the horizons of our thinking and to see everything from a universal perspective. In the same way as the Bible begins with a universal statement about God as the originator of everything through his creative act (Gen 1:1), it also concludes with some daring statements about how God unites himself to the one human family beyond the barriers of religions and nationalities. The author of the book of Revelation dwells on God's concluding union with humanity: "See the home of God is among humans. He will dwell with them as their God; they will be his peoples, and God himself will be with them. He will wipe away every tear from their eyes. Death will be no more; mourning and crying and pain will be nor more, for the first things have passed away" (Rev 21:3-4). Here we have a picture of the concluding act of God in relation to his kingdom and to the history which he has inaugurated. Beyond all philosophies and theologies, beyond all questions of orthodoxy and orthopraxis handled by religions and their promoters, God unites himself to the humankind which is the best form of religion, the finest form of union we can ever think of. In that final union of God and humankind the ultimate aspirations of every human soul will be fulfilled. *Nostra Aetate* has beautifully formulated this truth in the very beginning of that document: "For all peoples comprise a single community and have a single origin…One also is their final goal: God. His providence, his manifestations of goodness, and his saving designs extend to all men".[19] In his Encyclical *Fides et Ratio*, Pope John II speaks about the "universality of the human spirit, whose basic needs are the same in the most disparate cultures".[20] It is these universal and comprehensive considerations that have to be the main concerns of the Christian theologians and they need a shift of emphasis from their traditional approaches and theological positions to arrive at this new line of theological thinking and reflection.

---

[19] *NA* 1
[20] *FR 72*

www.ingramcontent.com/pod-product-compliance
Lightning Source LLC
Chambersburg PA
CBHW051941160426
43198CB00013B/2245